Aging in Place Conversations:
The Caregiver's Edition

Aging in Place Conversations: The Caregiver's Edition

National Aging in Place Council

Contributing Authors

Dr. Jocelyn Brown

Dr. Julie A. Brown

Dr. DeLon Canterbury

Mark Conacher

Dr. Israel Cross

James Donnelly

Sean Fitzgerald

Fritzi Gros-Daillon

Melanie Henry

Eve Hill

Gina Knight

Mary Lynch

Dr. Lydia Manning

Chris Orestis

Cindi Petito

Nicole Ramer

Felicia Saraceno

Jawbone Publishing   California   2025

Printed in the United States of America.
The content of *Aging in Place Conversations: The Caregiver's Edition* is for informational purposes only. It is not advice or guarantee of outcome. Information written, gathered, shared, and presented by the authors is their opinion and other resources provided are of reputable origination. The National Aging in Place Council and the authors are not responsible for errors or omissions in reporting or explanation. No individuals or industry professionals should use the information, resources, or tools contained herein for the purposes of self-diagnosis, self-treatment of any health-related condition or for financial or legal advice and strategies contained in this book without first consulting with your own healthcare professional, financial advisor, tax professional or conducting your own research and due diligence. The National Aging in Place Council and the authors of this book give no assurance or warranty regarding the accuracy, timeliness, or applicability of the content.

Library of Congress Cataloging-in-Publication Data Control Number:
Name: National Aging in Place Council
Title: Aging in Place Conversations: The Caregiver's Edition
Description: California, Jawbone Publishing, 2025|Includes bibliographical references.
Identifiers: ISBN: 978-1-59094-262-8
Subjects: Aging Parents, Aging, Eldercare, Aging in Place
Book cover design by APEX Media Solutions

Contents

Foreword v

Acknowledgments ix

How to Use This Book xi

Pillar 1: Housing

1 - 3 A.M. and Unprepared: A Caregiver's Awakening –
Mary Lynch 3
A late-night crisis sparks lessons on creating a safer and
more adaptable home.

2 - Caring Through Clutter: How Caregivers Can Create
a Safer, Simpler Home for Their Loved Ones – Nicole Ramer 19
Strategies for downsizing, reducing hazards, and honoring
family memories.

Pillar 2: Health & Wellness

3 - A Life Committed to Care – Sean Fitzgerald 41
Personal experiences and decades of professional work
helping older adults live safely at home.

4 - The Caregiver's Advantage: Ageism Awareness –
Eve Hill 57
Building an age-friendly home: How ageism influences caregiving
decisions and expectations.

5 - Technology-Supported Caregiving for Aging in Place –
Dr. Julie A. Brown and Dr. Jocelyn Brown 75
Explore how thoughtfully chosen technology can help
older adults stay safe and connected.

6 - Why Bathroom Safety Matters for Older Adults –
and Their Caregivers – Mark Conacher.. 91
Design solutions to prevent slips, falls, and injuries in
the bathroom.

7 - Aging in Place Starts in the Medicine Cabinet –
Dr. DeLon Canterbury... 109
How medication management and deprescribing
improve safety and quality of life.

8 - Aging in Motion: Staying Active with Mobility Supports? –
Cindi Petito 127
Choosing and using mobility aids to maintain independence
and community engagement.

9 - Resilient by Design: Emergency Planning for Aging
Communities – Felicia Saraceno 147
Practical steps to prepare for crises and recover
safely after emergencies.

Pillar 3: Finances

10 - Medicare: Does it Have to Be So Confusing? –
James Donnelly 157
A caregiver's guide to eligibility, enrollment, and
the importance of annual plan reviews.

11 - LTC-Life Settlements: Cashing Out Life Insurance Policies to
Age in Place – Chris Orestis 165
How life settlements can unlock funds for long-term care
and support at home.

Pillar 4: Transportation

12 - Driver Safety: A Caregiver's Guide – Melanie Henry 183
Discussing driving concerns—warning signs and steps to
making safe transitions from driving.

Pillar 5: Social Interaction

13 - Finding Strength from Afar – Fritzi Gros-Daillon 207
Practical strategies for long-distance caregiving and
staying connected.

14 - Balancing Personal and Professional Responsibilities:
Senior Life – Gina Knight & Dr. Lydia Manning 219
Managing work, family, and caregiving while preserving energy and well-
being.

What Should You Do Next? 235
Biographical Index of Contributing Authors..........................237
Endnotes and Additional Resources.....................................243

Foreword

Caring for an aging loved one is both one of the greatest privileges and one of the most complex responsibilities a person can take on. If you have opened this book, it means you are seeking guidance, encouragement, or simply the reassurance that you are not alone. This collection of wisdom and practical advice has been created for you, the caregiver, to make the path ahead a little clearer and the journey a little lighter.

Reframing Aging

Aging, in and of itself, is not a crisis. It is a natural and universal process - one we are fortunate to experience. Yet, social media and public conversations often frame it in crisis language with alarmist phrases such as: "The Silver Tsunami is coming" or "The Baby Boomers are getting older!" Such narratives distort a natural progression of life and rarely connect to constructive public health solutions.

Yes, our aging population is growing, but instead of panic, the conversation should shift toward: "That's why we need more long-term care solutions" or "What can we do to strengthen healthcare infrastructure and caregiving resources?" Too often, we fall back on oversimplified and misleading ideas about what it means to grow older, rather than focusing on real, meaningful solutions.

There is neither a magic curtain that drops at age 65, nor single age that defines capacity and purpose. This milestone is linked more to policy entitlements like Medicare or retirement than to an individual's health, purpose, or independence. Chronological age alone does not define a person's capacity to thrive. Research consistently shows that how we view aging deeply impacts health and well-being. Internalizing negative stereotypes can lead to poorer physical function, slower recovery, and even shorter life expectancy.

These distorted views affect not only individuals but also the systems and networks designed to support them. Increasingly, that support is provided outside of institutions - within people's homes and communities. This shift calls us to think differently about coordinated care, home safety, and environmental design. From grab bars to zero-step entries, accessible kitchens to smart technology, the right adjustments can turn the idea of aging in place from wishful thinking into a reality.

Centering Caregiving

Most aging adults prefer to remain in their own homes and communities safely and comfortably for as long as possible. But this does not happen by chance. It requires planning, resources, and often the unwavering support of family, friends, and frontline caregivers.

Today in the United States, more than 53 million people provide unpaid care to loved ones. Caregivers are essential partners in our healthcare system, complementing the central role aging adults play in directing their own lives and care. In addition to helping others navigate the healthcare system and serving older adults in daily activities, caregivers themselves may face enormous challenges in balancing work and family life, and managing the emotional weight of caregiving. I should also balance these statements by saying that caregiving can bring tremendous joy for both parties - it can strengthen relationships, bring shared laughter, and create lasting memories for both the caregiver and the person(s) receiving care.

Caregivers take many forms: spouses, adult children, grandchildren, siblings, neighbors, or even friends stepping in during times of need. Some live close by; others provide support from a distance. While the language we use to describe caregivers is evolving—care partner, care provider, carer - this book uses the term caregiver to honor all those offering their time, love, and energy so that older adults can age in place with dignity.

Why This Book Matters Now

This book, *Aging in Place Conversations: The Caregiver's Edition*, shines a light on the individuals and families making aging in place possible every day. It provides an accessible, reassuring guide for caregivers navigating the realities of supporting aging adults at home - or whatever "home" may look like.

Organized around the National Aging in Place Council's Five Pillars - Housing, Health & Wellness, Finances, Transportation, and Social Interaction - this book offers both practical tools and emotional encouragement. Its contributors include industry experts and caregivers themselves, blending professional insight with lived experience.

An Invitation to the Journey Ahead

If we want communities that truly support aging across the lifespan, we must design systems and resources that anticipate changing needs, rather than waiting for crisis moments. This book is part of that effort. It is meant to be read at your own pace, returned to often, and used as a reference whenever you need reassurance or guidance.

Think of these pages as companions on your journey - filled with wisdom, strategies, and reminders that you do not have to walk this path alone. Aging in place is not a single decision but a series of choices, made with care and foresight. With the right preparation and support, it can be not only possible but deeply fulfilling. I encourage you to take a pause at the end of each chapter and ask yourself, "What can I do with this information?" There is no need to rush, take your time to reflect. Our goal with this edition is to share stories that resonate, strategies you can put into practice, and support that help caregivers carry forward the critical work of aging in communities.

Israel Cross, PhD, ECHM, CAPS
President, National Aging in Place Council

Acknowledgments

We extend our heartfelt thanks to our team of contributing authors for generously sharing their time, expertise, and insight in bringing this book to life. Their diverse experiences, innovative ideas, and deep commitment to supporting older adults and their families form the foundation of this work. Together, they help bring light to pathways for creating meaningful plans to age in place with safety and choice. We also would like to thank Tara Ballman, CAPS, Executive Director of NAIPC, for her continued dedication to serving older adults and families through NAIPC's mission.

We are grateful to the following contributors:

Dr. Jocelyn Brown
Dr. Julie A. Brown
Dr. DeLon Canterbury
Mark Conacher
Dr. Israel Cross
James Donnelly
Sean Fitzgerald
Fritzi Gros-Daillon
Melanie Henry

Eve Hill
Gina Knight
Mary Lynch
Dr. Lydia Manning
Chris Orestis
Cindi Petito
Nicole Ramer
Felicia Saraceno

Most importantly, we thank you - our readers. As caregivers, this book was written with you in mind. Our goal is to equip you with knowledge and strategies so the later chapters of life for those you care for can be marked by safety, engagement, and meaningful choices. Just as importantly, we hope to provide information and resources that support you in this season of life, as you devote your energy to caring for loved ones.

Aging in Place Conversations: The Caregiver's Edition

We encourage you to share this book with those in your circle: family, friends, colleagues, and community leaders. Together, by pooling our experiences and working as a community, we can transform the vision of aging in place into a sustainable, empowering reality.

The National Aging in Place Council
www.AgeinPlace.org

How to Use This Book

Caring for a loved one - whether they live down the street or across the country - can be both deeply rewarding and surprisingly challenging. The demands of daily life, the emotional weight of responsibility, and the constant need to make the "right" decisions can feel overwhelming at times. This book is here to be your companion, your guide, and a source of encouragement as you navigate the caregiving journey.

The National Aging in Place Council is a network of professionals who provide resources and guidance on aging in place, using Five Pillars as a foundational framework: Housing, Health & Wellness, Finances, Transportation, and Social Interaction. There's no single way to read *Aging in Place Conversations: The Caregiver's Edition*, but you will notice that they are anchored in NAIPC's Five Pillars. You can approach it in the way that fits your life, your needs, and the challenges you face right now:

1. **Read it from beginning to end**. If you want the full story of caregiving, each chapter builds on the last, guiding you from understanding your role and recognizing strengths to managing long-distance challenges, balancing personal and professional responsibilities, and exploring available programs and resources. This way, you'll absorb the lessons and strategies in a natural flow.

2. **Focus on what matters most to you today**. Caregiving is unpredictable, and sometimes you need guidance for a specific challenge: a routine care decision, a crisis moment, or tips for preserving your own well-being. Other times, your focus may be broader, such as supporting a loved one living with dementia or building a reliable local support system.

The contents page includes chapter summaries, so you can quickly find the sections that speak to your situation and dive straight into the practical tools, strategies, and insights that will help you the most.

3. **Reflect and record**. Many chapters include prompts, checklists, or journaling suggestions. Keeping a notebook, notes app, or journal can help you capture insights, track wins, and plan your next steps. Reflection is not just about organizing tasks; it's about acknowledging the impact you are making, even from afar.

4. **Revisit this book often**. Your loved one's needs will change, and so will your role as a caregiver. Return to this book whenever new challenges arise, or when you simply need reassurance that you are not alone, that you are doing more than you realize, and that your care truly matters.

Above all, this book is written for you - the caregiver. Its authors share not only practical strategies but also the perspective, hope, and encouragement that come from real experience. Whether you read it cover to cover or pick the chapters you need most, the lessons in these pages are here to help you care with confidence, compassion, and grace - for both your loved one and yourself.

Pillar 1:
Housing

[1]

3 A.M. and Unprepared: A Caregiver's Awakening

by
Mary Lynch

It was 3 a.m. on a bitterly cold February morning in Baltimore. Inside my house, it felt just as frigid—the thermostat was set to nighttime savings mode, a habit I'd programmed years ago to keep energy costs down. The heat wouldn't kick on again until 5 a.m.

I was buried under layers of blankets, sound asleep, when a man's frantic screams jolted me awake. My heart pounded as I checked for an intruder. Then I realized... the sound was coming from the baby monitor on my nightstand.

In those disoriented moments, it hit me: my "babies" were in high school. The monitor wasn't for them - it was for our Pop.

William "Pop" Good had recently moved into my home. He was sleeping in a hospital bed we'd wedged into the dining room between the table and the hutch. It wasn't where I wanted him, just a rushed, makeshift setup—a temporary fix for a permanent problem in my not-so-age-friendly home. I threw the covers off and was on my feet before I even knew I was moving. When you're responsible for a loved one, instinct takes over. I don't know

if my feet even touched the steps on the way down. All I remember is
the sound of Pop's terrified voice and the pounding of my heart as I flew
toward him, thinking, "Is he okay? What am I about to find?"

Pop stood there in his boxer shorts, frantic and confused. His thin skin was
ice cold as I grabbed him, his arms flailing wildly, pushing me away in fear.
He fought me as I tried to steady him, his voice rising in panic, shouting
about water flooding the house. I held on, speaking softly, trying to break
through the fog, dressing him as gently but quickly as I could. Each button,
each sleeve, felt like a battle as I wrapped him in layers, hoping the warmth
would calm the storm inside him.

His eyes darted as if searching for an escape, and when I tried to reassure
him, he looked at me like I was a stranger. He wasn't here. In his mind,
water was pouring into the house. He shouted that we had to get out
before we drowned. Then, just as suddenly, his panic shifted—he was late
for a train, frantically searching for a bag he thought he needed to pack.

I'll never forget that moment. Watching my strong, steady grandfather -
the man who once captained boats on the Chesapeake Bay - suddenly lose
his bearings in his own mind broke me. He didn't recognize me. He was
terrified. A simple UTI had triggered hallucinations, and a wave of fear
and heartbreak crashed over me. It's impossible to describe the feeling of
realizing that someone you love more than life itself doesn't know who you
are.

And right then, I understood the hard truth: I was not prepared.
My home wasn't prepared.
None of us were.

Pop and the House That No Longer Fit

Pop wasn't just my grandfather; he was everything good in my life. William J. Good - his last name fit him like a badge of honor. I didn't know a better man. A salt-of-the-earth Baltimore native, Pop spent years as a captain and crabber, guiding his boat like it was an extension of himself. The only thing Pop loved more than Baltimore and the Bay was his family. He was my ride-or-die. My father figure. My number one guy.

Pop's row home - a classic 1950s Baltimore brick beauty - was his pride and joy. My father went to high school while living under that roof, I was bathed in the kitchen sink, and years later, my grandparents welcomed their great-grandchildren, my kids, into the very same home. I can still see myself as a little girl, lying on the living room floor with my head resting on the carpeted, single step up to the dining room, their poodle Pierre curled up beside me. Pop knew the placement of every single blade of his cherished Zoysia grass lawn. After 60 years in that home, every inch told a story. But homes built in that era weren't designed for the long lives we're living today. Back in 1950, life expectancy was nearly a decade shorter than it is now, according to the Social Security Administration. Pop had already lived 15 years beyond what was considered "normal" when his home was built. Today, with people living longer and healthier lives, homes often require updating to match those extended opportunities. As much as he loved that house, it simply wasn't built to support the later chapters of the life he was still living.

Both the front and rear entrances of the home required climbing stairs. The bedrooms and the only bathroom were tucked away on the third floor, while the laundry sat in the basement, accessible only by a narrow, steep staircase that could challenge even the surest footing. It never crossed my mind that the very place he loved most would one day no longer support his independence, creating challenges that forced him to adapt and ultimately step away from the life he had so carefully built there.

When his health declined, the only option was to bring him into my home. We cleared out the dining room—the place where family dinners and laughter once filled the air—and set up a hospital bed. Overnight, the heart of my home became a space of both care and quiet heartache. It wasn't perfect. It wasn't "age-friendly." But it was filled with love.

The Caregiving Wake-Up Call

We don't plan to be caregivers. One day, we simply wake up knee-deep in it—loving fiercely, juggling exhaustion, and wondering if we're doing any of it right.

Caregiving is full of contrasts. There are moments of pure grace—like when Pop's face lit up as the great-grands came home from school, eager to tell him about their day—and moments when the weight of responsibility felt almost unbearable. I've cried in my car, laughed in the middle of chaos, and prayed for just a few hours of sleep. Every single moment, no matter how hard, was stitched with love.

To anyone reading this who is a caregiver: I see you. I celebrate you. I champion you. Caregiving is beautiful, exhausting, heartbreaking, and love-filled work—and it is hard. My time with Pop was one of the greatest gifts of my life, but I won't pretend it was easy.

Yet alongside those challenges were moments I'll treasure forever. My children saw firsthand what it means to honor your elders and what generational love truly looks like. They got to love their Pop in a way that shaped who they are—and I'll always be grateful for that gift.

Pop passed peacefully—just three days after we celebrated his 84th birthday with a house full of family, a few of his lifelong childhood friends who had outlived so many others, and a whole lot of love as we sang "Happy Birthday" and shared strawberry shortcake. It's a memory I'll always hold close.

Caring for Pop taught me lessons no book or class could ever teach. It showed me that caregiving isn't just about managing someone's day—it's about creating an environment where they can still feel safe, dignified, and at home. And that's when I realized this is where my two worlds— caregiving and real estate—collide.

After nearly three decades in real estate, my biggest gift to other caregivers isn't just empathy—it's expertise. I know how much the right home (or the right modifications) can lighten the load, reduce stress, and keep everyone safer. Because of what I went through with Pop, I've made it my mission to guide families through the tough housing decisions—whether that's aging in place, downsizing, or finding something that truly feels like home.

A Mission Born from Heartbreak

That night—barefoot, heart pounding, holding my trembling grandfather—I had a realization that shook me to my core: I was unprepared. My home was unprepared. And suddenly, the term "forever home"—one I'd used for two decades in my real estate career—felt hollow.

At 3 a.m., I saw it with new eyes: most homes aren't built to be "forever" homes at all. In fact, according to the 2020 U.S. Census, only 10% of housing units in the United States have a step-free entryway, a bedroom and full bathroom on the first floor, and at least one accessibility feature— such as handrails or a built-in shower seat. That single statistic hit me like a brick: how could we keep calling homes "forever" when, so few are built to carry us through every chapter of life?

For over 20 years, I'd prided myself on being a matchmaker—finding not just houses, but the perfect homes where families could build their lives. I believed I was guiding them into their next joyful chapter, handing them the keys to their "forever home." But standing in my dining room that night, I felt a sharp frustration with my own profession. How often do we ask, "What happens when you—or a loved one—can't do the stairs anymore?" How often do we talk about accessibility, planning, or what "forever" really means? The truth is, we don't—and I vowed, right then and there, to change that.

That 3 a.m. moment didn't just change me as a granddaughter; it shifted me as a professional and as a human being. I understood that homes must evolve to support the people who live in them—not just for today's needs, but for every chapter of life.

This realization became my mission. I've taken my passion for real estate and turned it into advocacy for better housing for older adults and accessible home design. I'm proud that Maryland recently passed legislation I championed to expand housing options for older adults and families. And in 2024, I founded the Greater Baltimore Chapter of the National Aging in Place Council (NAIPC), where we've built an incredible professional community resource group—a network of trusted experts and advocates—dedicated to educating our community on aging safely, with dignity, and with options.

If love could build a ramp, I would have built one a mile long for my grandfather. Instead, I built a mission. A mission that is GOOD—in honor of William Good and the life he lived so fully. I know he's proud. With every family I help, I see his smile and feel that bigger-than-life hug, reminding me why this work matters.

What Makes a Home for all Stages of Life?

Pop's home taught me a hard truth: a house isn't truly a *forever home* unless it can carry you through all of life's stages—not just the easy chapters. Most of us don't think about this until a crisis forces us to. We buy homes for the life we have now -close to schools, with big backyards, and plenty of stairs to keep us moving. But as life shifts, those same stairs and narrow hallways can become daily hurdles.

A forever home is about more than style or square footage; it's about safety, adaptability, and peace of mind. After caregiving for Pop, I've come to believe that there are a few key features every home should have if you want to live fully and independently, no matter what the future holds.

3 Game-Changers for Every Home:

Main-Level Living: Having a bedroom, bathroom, and laundry on one level makes life easier now—and crucial later if climbing stairs becomes a challenge.

No-Step Entry: One step-free entrance or the ability to add a ramp isn't just for wheelchairs: it's for anyone carrying groceries, strollers, or recovering from an injury.

Curbless Showers and Wide Doorways: A walk-in shower with room for a bench, paired with 36" doorways, makes homes safer and more welcoming for everyone.

Note: To download a free guide to future-proofing your own home, including the full checklist of 12 features I recommend for a Forever Home, visit www.downsizingbaltimore.com to get a copy of *Forever Home Playbook*.

Right-Sizing: Creating More, Not Less

Right-sizing—or downsizing, as most people call it—has nothing to do with giving up. It's not about moving to "less"; it's about creating more.

More freedom.
More energy for what matters most.
More time spent living—not cleaning, fixing, or worrying.

The truth is a home that once felt perfect can quietly become a burden. The stairs that were never an issue start to feel like a mountain. Rooms that once held laughter and family now sit empty, collecting dust and memories. And while those memories are beautiful, they don't need a big, complicated house to keep them alive.

When I think about right-sizing, I think about the clients and families I've helped who found joy—not loss—in making the move.

Right-sizing is about gaining freedom from things that no longer serve you:

- **Freedom from maintenance** that steals your weekends.
- **Freedom from financial drain**, like heating and cooling unused rooms.
- **Freedom from fear and uncertainty** - whether it is the fear of falling on stairs or the uncertainty of living alone in a house that feels too overwhelming.

The key is to start before a crisis forces your hand. The earlier you plan, the more options you have, and the more control you keep over your future.

Real People, Real Moves: Case Studies in Rightsizing

Over the years, I've walked alongside incredible clients as they've navigated the emotional and practical challenges of finding a "next right home." Each story is unique, but they all share one truth: moving doesn't have to mean giving something up—it can mean gaining more.

Case #1: Tony & Peg's Villa Life – Letting Go of the "Forever Home"

After 35 years in their big colonial, Tony and Peg found that the upkeep had become overwhelming. The yard work, the stairs, and the endless list of home maintenance started to chip away at their energy. They decided it was time to simplify.

We explored several options, and when they walked into a single-level villa, something clicked. The open layout, the bright rooms, and the low-maintenance lifestyle felt like freedom. Within a month of moving, Peg told me: "We should have done this five years ago."

Now, their weekends are spent with grandkids or exploring new hobbies, not mowing lawns or fixing leaky gutters.

Takeaway: Tony and Peg's story reminds us that a smaller home can give you a bigger life.

Case #2: Sue's New Chapter – Trading Space for Sunshine

Sue, a widow in her late 70s, knew her two-story home no longer served her. The stairs hurt her knees, the large rooms felt empty, and the upkeep weighed her down emotionally. We looked at several places, but when she stepped into a condo with a sunroom, she stopped in her tracks.
"I feel lighter," she said, beaming as she stood in the sunroom that instantly felt like hers.

It wasn't just about downsizing; it was about finding a space that matched her life and energy. With less to maintain and more light filling her days,

Sue has started gardening in pots on her balcony and hosting small brunches in her new sunroom.

Takeaway: Sue's move is proof that the right home can bring not just peace of mind, but joy.

Case #3: John's 5-Star Upgrade – From Isolation to Connection

John lived in a third-floor condo with no elevator. Every trip up and down felt like a challenge, and after a fall, his family urged him to consider a continuing care community. He was reluctant at first—he thought he'd be losing independence.

But then came the food. The first time he tasted one of the community's chef-prepared meals, his eyes lit up.

"These meals are better than any restaurant in town," he now says, proudly sharing that he hasn't eaten alone once since moving.

His days are filled with conversation, friendships, and activities he didn't know he was missing.

Takeaway: John's story shows that the right move can mean trading isolation for connection and purpose.

Case #4: The Creative Solution – Donna's Backyard Independence

When one family realized their aging mother, Donna, needed to be closer but still valued her independence, they took a creative approach. They built an Accessory Dwelling Unit (ADU)—a "granny pod"—in their backyard.

It's a small but fully equipped home, just steps away from the main house. Donna has her own kitchen and living room, but she's close enough for family meals, grandkids' visits, and daily check-ins.

"It's the best decision we ever made," her daughter told me.

Donna loves having her independence while feeling the warmth and security of being near her family.

Takeaway: Creative solutions like ADUs can give aging parents independence and keep families close.

Case #5: Carol & Mike – Thriving by Right-Sizing Early

Carol and Mike, both in their early 60s, made what friends called a "radical" decision—they sold their large home before retirement.

"We didn't want to wait until a health issue forced us to move," Mike explained.

We found them a single-level home in a vibrant 55+ community with a clubhouse, pickleball courts, and neighbors who quickly became friends. They now spend their time traveling, socializing, and focusing on what truly matters, free from the stress of a large house.

Takeaway: Carol and Mike's story proves that right-sizing early can give you more energy to enjoy the best years ahead.

Case #6: Margaret – A Lesson in Waiting Too Long

Margaret, 84, held tightly to her family home for over 50 years. She always said, "I'll never leave this house." Then a sudden fall on the stairs changed everything. Her children were left scrambling—cleaning, repairing, and preparing the home for sale—while also managing her care and finances. "I wish I'd made this decision on my own terms instead of waiting for an accident to make it for me," she admitted later.

Margaret's story is one I share often because it's not just about her—it's about the gift of planning ahead.

Takeaway: Waiting too long can turn a joyful choice into a crisis. Plan now, while you still have choices.

Case Study Reflection

These stories highlight a simple truth: the size of your home doesn't measure the size of your life. Right-sizing isn't about loss; it's about gaining freedom, joy, and peace of mind. Whether it's simplifying life, finding community, or exploring creative solutions like an ADU, the key is to start while you still have the energy, options, and excitement to embrace your next chapter—on your own terms.

Up next: The Weight of Stuff—because for most people, the hardest part of moving isn't the new home...it's deciding what to take with you, what to let go of, and how to honor a lifetime of memories without drowning in them.

The Weight of Stuff

According to a 2014 *Los Angeles Times* article, the average American home contains more than 300,000 items. Every single one of those things requires attention—dusting, moving, storing, or at the very least, keeping track of.

We hold onto these items because they remind us of people, places, or moments. But the truth is, not all of them deserve equal space in our lives—or our closets.

Here's the hard question I ask clients: *"Which pieces tell your story? Which ones would you want your children or grandchildren to hold on to?"*

If everything is labeled "special," nothing truly is. The key is to highlight the items that really matter. Display the heirloom china that makes you smile every time you see it. Frame the love letters or wedding photos. Give those pieces a place of honor—and let go of the rest with gratitude.

I like to think of right-sizing not as letting go, but as curating your life. And yes, I know the thought of tackling closets and attics full of memories can feel like moving a mountain. But here's the truth: the memories aren't in the things. They live in you. They're in the stories you tell at the dinner table, in the traditions you pass down, in the way you make your family feel loved.

If you're feeling stuck, start small. One drawer. One closet. One decision. The best time to make life easier was yesterday. The second-best time is today.

If Only I Could Have Guided Pop Sooner

If only I could have guided Pop to make these choices earlier. If only I'd known then what I know now—about safe housing, about planning ahead, about how much easier life could have been for both of us if his home had fit his needs instead of fighting against them.

Pop's row home was his pride and joy, but as the years went on, it posed more daily challenges than comforts. I found myself increasingly aware of the small things – the stairs, the rugs, the narrow doorways – everyday tasks that once seemed effortless but now required more care.

But he loved that house fiercely, and I didn't yet have the language—or maybe the courage—to gently show him that loving a home doesn't mean you have to stay in it forever. I wish I could have helped him see that letting go of the house wouldn't have meant letting go of the memories. Those would always be his.

What About You?

Does your home still fit the life you're living now—or the life you want for the next chapter? Or are you holding on because of the memories, the "just in case" moments, or because the thought of letting go feels too overwhelming?

Here's the truth I wish someone had told me earlier: staying in a home that no longer fits often leads to more than just inconvenience. When a home is too big or too demanding, small repairs become big ones, rooms sit unused, and the costs of maintaining it quietly drain your energy and your wallet. Worse, the longer we wait, the more likely it is that our families will one day have to step in during a crisis—when emotions are high and decisions are harder.

You Deserve a Home That Loves You Back

You deserve a home that supports you, not one that silently challenges you with every step or task. A home that doesn't just hold your memories but holds you—safely, comfortably, and with dignity.
If there's one thing I wish I could tell Pop now, it's this: choosing a home that fits your life today doesn't erase the past—it honors it. Every memory he made in that row home would have come with him, no matter where he lived.

That's why I share his story. I don't want anyone else to wait too long, to struggle in a house that no longer serves them, or to feel trapped by the weight of "stuff" or the fear of change.

Think Beyond the Obvious

Sometimes, it's the little things that make a home "future-ready." Is there room to add a laundry station on the main level if carrying baskets up and down stairs becomes too much? Could the kitchen layout allow someone to cook or prep meals while seated? Is there a quiet space that could double as a home office—or even a caregiving hub—down the road?

The goal isn't to predict every scenario—it's to choose a home that supports your life story, no matter the chapter. Small, thoughtful features today—like a curbless shower or a level entry—can prevent big headaches later.

Want to see the full "12 Features of a Forever Home Every Buyer Should Consider?" Download my Forever Home Playbook at www.downsizingbaltimore.com.

Closing Takeaway

The truth is, "forever" isn't about staying in the same house forever—it's about building a life in a home that grows with you, supports you, and makes every season of life easier, not harder. Whether that means adapting the space you have, right-sizing to something that fits you better, or planning for future needs, the goal is the same: to live freely, safely, and without regret.

Carrying Pop's Legacy Forward

I often think about that night—the fear in Pop's eyes, the heartbreak of realizing that neither of our homes could truly support him in his final chapter. I also think about the quiet moments of grace we shared in my dining room-turned-care room, the conversations that mattered most, the love that needed no words.

Every family I help, every conversation I start about aging well, is a tribute to William Good. His name was more than a name—it was who he was. Everything I do now, I do in honor of him. This mission is GOOD.

Pop taught me that love is not just about showing up in the moment— it's about preparing for the moments to come. That's why I advocate for accessible homes, for open conversations about aging, and for making choices today that protect dignity tomorrow.

Whether you're caring for someone you love, proactively right-sizing to a home that fits your next chapter or guiding others as a professional—you have the chance to plan for more than a house. You have the chance to build a legacy of comfort, safety, and love.

Because in the end, it's not just about finding a place to live—it's about creating a life you love, in a home that loves you back.

If you're standing at a crossroads, wondering if your home still fits your life, consider this: Every step you take to plan now is a gift to your future self— and to the people who love you. Don't wait for a crisis to make the call.

Thank you for letting me share Pop's story with you. I hope it inspires you to think not just about where you live, but about how you want to live— and the legacy of comfort and love you want to leave behind. Forever isn't a place—it's the life you build. Start designing the home and future you deserve before life decides for you.

[2]

Caring Through Clutter:
How Caregivers Can Create a Safer, Simpler Home for Their Loved Ones

by
Nicole Ramer

Caring for an aging loved one is an emotional and physical journey, and one of the most significant challenges caregivers face is managing the clutter that often accumulates in the home. Over the years, objects pile up – papers, furniture, keepsakes, and countless other items – and before long, the home that was once a comfortable sanctuary becomes overwhelming.

For caregivers, this clutter is more than just an inconvenience. It creates safety hazards, increases stress levels, and hinders the ability to manage daily tasks. Decluttering isn't just about clearing space – it's about creating a safer, calmer environment that allows both the caregiver and their loved one to thrive.

This chapter will guide you through the process of caring through clutter – helping you understand how to approach decluttering in a way that is both empathetic and practical. Whether you're managing your loved one's home or preparing for a future transition, the tips, resources, and strategies in this chapter will help you reduce overwhelm and create a living space that's safe, organized, and conducive to peaceful aging-in-place.

Understanding the Emotional Weight of 'Stuff'

Imagine a caregiver sitting beside their aging parent, surrounded by stacks of items. The parent clutches an old, faded photograph of their late spouse. The caregiver suggests, "We need to clear some of this out; it's taking up too much space." The parent's face tightens. It's not just a photo; it's a memory – and so is everything else in the room.

Decluttering is one of the most emotionally challenging tasks caregivers face. For many older adults, their home is more than just a space – it's a repository of memories. Each item, from family heirlooms to photos, holds meaning, symbolizing experiences, losses, and love. These possessions are tied to identity, history, and relationships, and parting with them can feel like letting go of a piece of oneself.

Emotional Attachment to Possessions

The first step in decluttering is acknowledging and respecting these emotions. For older adults, especially those with cognitive changes or dementia, letting go can be frightening. It may feel like erasing their past. As caregivers, it's essential to make this process gentle and compassionate, creating a safe space for the older adult to express their feelings without judgment.

For example, I worked with a family where the father had lived in the same home for over 40 years. When it came time to sort through his things, he was reluctant to part with a collection of old, worn tools that had been passed down from his father. They weren't functional anymore, but they held deep emotional significance. His daughter said, "I understand why he wants to keep them, but I can't imagine them fitting in his new place." By taking the time to listen to his stories about each tool, we helped him let go, piece by piece, while honoring the memories attached to them.

Tip:
Use the "Keep, Share, Honor" method:
• **Keep the essentials** and items that serve a functional purpose.
• **Share sentimental items** with family, letting them appreciate the memories now.
• **Honor the memories** by creating a memory box, digitizing photos, or repurposing fabrics into quilts or keepsakes to preserve the stories without the physical burden.

Tip:
Ask open-ended questions to encourage reflection:
• "What does this item mean to you?"
• "What memories does this photograph hold?"

These questions help your loved one engage with the emotional side of letting go, without feeling their memories are being dismissed.

The Emotional Decluttering Process

Decluttering a loved one's home is as much an emotional process as it is a physical one. To approach it with compassion, take time to validate their feelings and engage in conversations that allow them to share the stories behind their belongings. For a more detailed guide and resources on navigating emotional attachment during the decluttering process, scan the QR code below to access a helpful DOC with additional tips and strategies.

Prioritizing Safety Without Overwhelming Change
The Hidden Dangers of Clutter

Clutter can be a serious safety hazard, especially for aging adults with mobility issues, vision problems, or changes in cognition. It's easy to overlook how cluttered environments can impact a person's well-being, but for older adults, it's a real threat. According to the U.S. Centers for Disease Control and Prevention (CDC), falls are the leading cause of injury for adults ages 65 and older. Clutter – loose rugs, crowded walkways, and disorganized furniture – contributes significantly to these accidents. In addition to physical hazards, clutter can cause mental confusion and anxiety, particularly for those with cognitive impairments.

The good news is that prioritizing safety doesn't require overwhelming changes. Small, intentional adjustments can improve the environment without completely altering the space your loved one knows and feels comfortable in.

I recall working with Carla, a caregiver for her father, Bill, who lived with mild dementia. His living room was cluttered with overstuffed furniture and surfaces full of items, which made it difficult for him to move around safely. After one fall, Carla realized that she needed to make changes for his safety.

Tip:
Start with high-risk areas, like hallways, kitchens, and bathrooms. Focus on removing tripping hazards, such as loose rugs and excess furniture. Simple updates like adding grab bars, motion-sensor lights, and reconfiguring furniture to create clear walking paths can significantly improve safety.

Tip: Create a home safety checklist that includes:
• Reorganizing frequently used items for easy access.
• Securing furniture to walls to prevent tipping.
• Removing obstacles that might hinder mobility.

For people living with dementia, clutter not only causes physical hazards but also increases cognitive confusion. Simplifying the environment can make it easier for them to navigate, reducing anxiety and promoting independence. For example, Carla rearranged Bill's living room, creating a more open space that allowed him to move comfortably. She cleared counters of dangerous items, like cleaning products and medications, which helped lower his anxiety and boosted his confidence.

Tip:
Involve your loved one in the process. Ask them where they feel safest and what items they would like to keep or remove. This gives them agency over the changes and helps them feel in control of their environment.

To help you implement these home safety priorities with ease, I've provided a downloadable DOC that includes a printable checklist and additional resources to guide you through the process. Scan the QR code below to access the document, and use it to take actionable steps toward creating a safer living space for your loved one. This resource will help you stay organized and focused as you make small yet impactful changes to improve safety without overwhelming your loved one.

The 5-Minute Decluttering Rule

One of the biggest challenges in caregiving is managing the time needed for daily responsibilities. Between medical appointments, medication schedules, meal preparation, and emotional support, there often isn't time to declutter the whole house. But I've found that small, focused efforts can lead to major results. That's where the 5-minute rule comes in.

Tip:
Instead of setting aside hours, set a timer for just five minutes each day. The key here is consistency. Over time, these short bursts of decluttering will add up, leaving you with an organized and safer environment. Focus on one area – whether it's a single drawer, a shelf, or a countertop. Even five minutes is enough to clear a small area, and that's a great first step.

For example, Elizabeth, a client of mine, found that using the 5-minute rule worked wonders in her caregiving routine. Between caring for her mother and managing her own busy life, Elizabeth didn't have time to declutter for hours. She started with just 5 minutes a day, targeting one small area of the home. She found that these small actions helped her maintain order and prevented the clutter from piling up.

Tip:
Create a donation box and keep it near your workspace. As you declutter for those 5 minutes, immediately place unwanted items in the donation box. Take immediate action by donating or discarding items right after the session, which ensures that nothing piles up again. It's essential to keep the momentum going, no matter how small.

Tip:
If your loved one is capable, invite them to participate in the 5-minute session. Even if they only help for a few minutes, the process can increase

their sense of involvement and empower them to make decisions about what stays and what goes.

By following the 5-Minute Decluttering Rule, you can tackle small tasks and make consistent progress toward a more organized home. Each 5-minute session allows you to focus on one area at a time, making decluttering less overwhelming and more achievable. To help you stay on track and make the most of your time, scan the QR code below for a printable DOC with additional tips and resources on how to use this method effectively.

Downsizing in Stages: The "Keep, Share, Honor" Method

When downsizing, especially after decades of living in the same home, the task can feel insurmountable. However, downsizing doesn't have to be done all at once. By breaking the process into smaller, manageable stages, caregivers can help their loved ones ease into the transition.

Tip:
Start with the essentials – items that are used regularly. Ask questions such as:
"Does this fit the life you are living now?"
"Have you used this item in the past year?"
"Do you still need this piece of furniture for daily living?"

This helps your loved one evaluate each item based on functionality. Once the essentials are sorted, move on to sentimental items. This step is often the most challenging, but by approaching it gradually, it becomes less overwhelming. Help them understand that memories can be honored without keeping everything.

For example, Julie, a caregiver for her father, spent several months working with him to downsize after he moved into a senior living community. Julie started by going through clothing and kitchenware, and after that, they tackled family photos and memorabilia. Instead of forcing her father to part with cherished items, Julie helped him share them with family members, creating new memories and connections while reducing the clutter.

Tip:
Honor memories by turning photos into digital albums or creating memory quilts from old clothes. This allows your loved one to preserve the emotional connection to these items without keeping them physically.

Downsizing doesn't need to be done all at once. By breaking it down into stages, the process becomes more manageable and less emotionally overwhelming. The Keep, Share, Honor method helps you decide which items are worth keeping, which should be shared with loved ones, and which should be honored creatively.

For more detailed guidance and additional tips on downsizing in stages, scan the QR code below to access a printable DOC that will help you stay organized and focused throughout the process. This will give you extra tools and resources for making the transition smoother and more thoughtful.

Creating Organizational Systems That Stick

An organized home doesn't have to be perfectly neat, but it should be functional and easy to navigate, especially when you're a caregiver managing multiple responsibilities. The goal is to create systems that work for both you and your loved one, allowing you to find what you need quickly and easily without adding extra stress.

Tip:
Start by creating clear and simple systems that make sense for your loved one's lifestyle and needs. For example, use clear bins for storing seasonal clothing, and label them so items can be easily identified. Use open shelving in areas like the kitchen and bathroom so frequently used items are visible and accessible.

In many cases, the simpler the system, the better it works. Overcomplicating storage can lead to frustration for both the caregiver and the person being cared for. For example, some older adults may struggle to understand complicated storage systems, so simplicity is key.

The Command Center: A Caregiver's Best Friend

One effective strategy for organization is creating a Command Center – a central hub where you store all the important documents, such as medical records, appointments, grocery lists, and emergency contacts. The idea is to have everything in one place so that you can stay on top of caregiving tasks without feeling overwhelmed.

For instance, Nancy, a caregiver for her aging mother, created a Command Center in her kitchen. She used a wall-mounted calendar to keep track of medical appointments, a binder for storing important documents, and a folder for bills and receipts. This system helped her feel more organized and reduced the stress of constantly searching for documents or missing appointments.

Tip:
Keep the Command Center as simple as possible. Use color-coded folders or labels to separate categories like medications, appointments, and financial documents. Make sure the center is located in a place where both you and your loved one can easily access it.

Tip:
Consider adding a weekly review to your Command Center routine. Every Sunday evening, take a few minutes to check the appointments for the week, confirm medication schedules, and make any adjustments to the calendar. This regular check-in will help reduce confusion and make the caregiving process feel less stressful.

For a more detailed, interactive guide to creating lasting organizational systems, scan the QR code below to access a printable DOC with additional resources, tips, and advice to help you build systems that work for your space and lifestyle.

Letting Go Without Guilt

One of the most difficult emotional hurdles for caregivers is guilt. It's a common feeling when helping your loved one part with items they've held dear for years. Many caregivers feel that they are somehow betraying their loved one's memories or erasing their identity by suggesting they let go of possessions.

But here's the truth:
Letting go of physical items doesn't diminish the memories attached to them. In fact, letting go can make room for more important aspects – like safety, peace of mind, and quality of life. When we part with non-essential items, we make space for the things that truly matter: health, comfort, and connection.

Tip:
Reframe the process of letting go by focusing on the positive outcomes of decluttering, such as improved safety, reduced anxiety, and the creation of a peaceful, manageable living space. Instead of thinking about what is being

lost, focus on what is being gained – a safer home, a clearer mind, and a more organized space that enhances quality of life.

For example, I worked with Lena, a caregiver who had been helping her mother move to an assisted living community. At first, Lena struggled with her mother's attachment to various family items. However, after a few difficult but compassionate conversations, Lena helped her mom understand that letting go of things wasn't a way of erasing memories but a way to make room for new experiences and memories. By focusing on the practical benefits – like a more functional and safer space – Lena was able to ease her mother's guilt and make the process more manageable.

Tip:
Help your loved one reframe the situation by saying things like, "We're not getting rid of memories; we're making space for new memories," or "Let's keep the memories alive in a way that's more manageable."

Tip:
Take breaks when guilt sets in. If the process becomes too emotional or overwhelming for either you or your loved one, step back for a moment. It's important to acknowledge the emotional difficulty of the task, but it's also crucial to keep the bigger picture in mind. This space is meant to serve your loved one's needs – it's not about minimizing their past but about empowering their future.

For more detailed guidance on handling emotional attachment and guilt throughout the process, scan the QR code below to access a printable DOC that includes additional tools, resources, and strategies to make the decluttering process as smooth and compassionate as possible.

Downsizing and Moving: Packing With the Unpack in Mind™

Moving can be stressful, especially when downsizing to a smaller space. One of the best ways to make the process easier is to embrace the concept of Packing With the Unpack in Mind™. This framework ensures that only necessary items are packed, and it helps streamline the transition to a new home.

Tip:
Before starting to pack, measure the new space – get a floor plan and understand the limitations of the new home. Determine how much space is available for furniture and belongings. This will help you make decisions about what items will fit and what should be left behind.

As Mary Kay Buysee, NASMM's Executive Director, points out:

"For adults who have lived in their homes for 30 or 40 years, it's more than just a move. Most older adults making this type of transition need to downsize considerably. The organizational and physical tasks – whether

you are moving or downsizing to stay in the home – can be overwhelming. Families need a professional to provide them with the necessary tools essential to reduce the stress that can accompany this type of move – and that's exactly what we do!"

This quote speaks to the heart of the downsizing process. When preparing for a move, caregivers must help their loved ones let go of items that are no longer needed or practical. Downsizing is emotionally challenging, but it's a necessary step to make the transition to a smaller space more manageable and comfortable.

Step-by-step packing tips:
Sort through each category of items – clothing, kitchenware, furniture, decor, etc.
Measure your furniture to see if it will fit in the new space.
Create a floor plan to map out where each piece of furniture will go.
Let go of things that don't serve a practical or emotional purpose.

By letting go of unnecessary items and focusing on only the essential, you ensure the transition is more manageable, and your loved one's new home remains comfortable, functional, and safe. For further guidance on the downsizing and moving process, scan the QR code below to access a printable DOC with additional tips, packing strategies, and tools that will help you complete the move smoothly and without overwhelming stress.

Value of Items that Can Be Sold – Expectations Versus Reality

When people begin the process of downsizing, many assume that the items in the home, especially antiques, collectibles, and furniture, will sell for more than they actually do. It's a common mistake to overestimate the value of these items and underestimate the time and effort required to sell them.

The reality is that market forces largely dictate the price of an item once you decide to sell it. As Barry Gordon, a leading expert in senior downsizing and the Founder of MaxSold, emphasizes:

"Your items are worth whatever you want them to be worth so long as you are not trying to sell them. Once you decide you are selling the items, their monetary value is largely determined by forces other than you."

This philosophy highlights a fundamental truth about selling household goods: the value of an item is not solely based on its sentimental or historical significance, but on market demand, condition, and buyer interest. What seems invaluable in your eyes may only hold modest value for others, and finding the right buyer may take time and effort.

It's not unusual for items to take months to sell at the price you want. And even then, you might find that the value of certain items doesn't match the effort it takes to find the right buyer.

For example, Ellen, one of my clients, believed that her mother's antique dining table was worth thousands of dollars. After months of listing it online and holding garage sales, she eventually sold it for a fraction of the price. Understanding market value and setting realistic expectations from the start can save a lot of frustration.

Tip:
Before listing items for sale, take some time to research their value. You can check online auction sites like eBay or MaxSold to get a sense of what similar items have sold for recently. Hiring an appraiser for high-value or antique items can help you set a realistic price.

Tip:
If you're feeling overwhelmed by the thought of selling items, consider working with a professional who specializes in estate sales or online auctions. They have experience in pricing, selling, and managing the logistics of the entire process, saving you time and ensuring that the sale is handled efficiently.

Working with a REALTOR® – Listing and Selling the House Should Come Last

When it's time to sell a loved one's home, caregivers often feel pressure to move quickly, especially due to the need for funds. Living costs for older adults are high, and families often rely on the proceeds from the home sale to cover the move and care expenses.

However, selling the house should come last – after the contents have been sorted and the home is prepared. Rushing to list the property can cause stress, especially if the home sells quickly, leaving little time to manage belongings. This leads to chaos, making the transition more difficult. Rushing can also lead to physical strain, emotional stress, and health risks. The pressures of packing, decision-making, and the emotional toll can seriously affect the caregiver's health.

Decluttering and downsizing should be the first priority. By organizing and clearing the space first, caregivers can make thoughtful decisions without being pressured by a looming sale.

While it may seem tempting to move everything into storage, this often complicates the process. Without a clear plan, moving unorganized items can create more chaos.

As Katherine Ambrose, America's Senior Home Coach™, often shares with families: "Downsizing should leave you OVERJOYED, not overwhelmed."

Her advice emphasizes thoughtful preparation. By focusing on right-sizing the current home and planning for the new space, you'll create a smoother, less stressful transition.

Preparing the Home for Sale – Without Rushing

Instead of rushing the sale, focus on decluttering and downsizing first. This gives everyone more time to make informed decisions, ensuring a smoother transition for both the caregiver and the older adult.

Here are the key steps to take when preparing the house:
- **Declutter and Organize:** Start by removing unnecessary items. Tackle one room at a time. Consider creating a decision box for items you're unsure about.
- **Rightsize for the New Home:** Measure the new space and decide what fits. Plan to take only the essentials.
- **Repairs and Updates**: Once decluttered, make necessary repairs – patch walls, fix minor plumbing, and add fresh paint.
- **Clear Paths for REALTOR® Success:** By the time the REALTOR® gets involved, the home should be clean, organized, and ready for viewing. This allows the REALTOR® to focus on selling the property, not managing clutter.

Sources and How to Find Help

For Senior Move Management®: www.NASMM.org
If readers are looking for professional move management services that
specialize in helping older adults declutter, downsize, and move, the
National Association of Senior & Specialty Move Managers (NASMM)
website is a valuable resource. They have a searchable directory of Certified
Senior Move Managers® (SMM~C) who can assist with the entire moving
and downsizing process. NASMM-certified professionals are trained
to work with older adults and understand the emotional and physical
challenges of moving, making them a trusted choice for families.

For Professional Organizing: www.NAPO.net
Similarly, for readers looking to hire professional organizers to help with
decluttering and creating systems in the home, the National Association
of Productivity & Organizing Professionals (NAPO) is a great resource.
NAPO offers a directory of Certified Professional Organizers® (CPO®),
who specialize in organizing spaces to suit the needs of older adults and
their families. These experts can assist with everything from general
decluttering to creating systems for aging-in-place.

Conclusion

Caring for a loved one through clutter is not just about organizing a home
– it's about creating a safe, functional environment that allows both the
caregiver and the older adult to feel at ease. Clutter can present emotional
and physical obstacles, but it can also be a sign that something deeper
is at play – often the unseen weight of a lifetime's worth of possessions.
Addressing this clutter is one of the first steps in fostering a safe,
manageable, and peaceful living space for an aging loved one.

Sometimes, decluttering and downsizing don't happen in a vacuum. For many families, downsizing and moving are not just future considerations but urgent, necessary actions in the face of safety concerns. One fall can significantly alter the course of a person's life, daily routines, and independence, making proactive safety planning especially important. A sudden fall can result in hospitalization, rehabilitation, and, ultimately, a move to a safer living environment – often at the most overwhelming moment of their lives.

Unfortunately, most older adults and their families are not prepared for this type of transition. When someone can no longer safely care for themselves in their longtime home – the one they planned to age in or die in – decluttering, downsizing, moving, and resettling must happen all at once. It's a massive undertaking that combines both the emotional and physical ties of letting go of a lifetime of possessions while trying to make sense of a new chapter in their life.

This is why the discussions around downsizing, moving, and selling the family home were necessary topics for this chapter. While these may seem like logistical concerns, they are inextricably linked to caregiving and caring through clutter. By preparing early – even if a move is not imminent – you can avoid the stress and chaos that often accompany sudden, rushed transitions. When you start the process of decluttering and downsizing early, you not only protect your loved one's emotional well-being but also give yourself the space to make thoughtful decisions about their future care.

Taking action now, while the clutter is still manageable, sets both you and your loved one up for a future that is safe, calm, and empowering. Whether it's clearing out unnecessary items, ensuring that the new home is ready, or making a smooth transition when the time comes, the goal is the same: to make the home as clutter-free as possible, leaving your loved one feeling supported and cared for every step of the way.

Pillar 2:
Health & Wellness

[3]

A Life Committed to Care

by
Sean Fitzgerald

"Aging in place starts with the home™" isn't just a tagline at TruBlue Home Service Ally — it's a principle, and one that my career, focus and passion revolves around. Why? Our aging population deserves respect, comfort, and dignity.

After decades spent working alongside older adults, their families, and the professionals who care for them, I believe in this statement deeply. Here's why.

Over the past twenty years, I've devoted my career to understanding what it really takes for older adults to live not just longer, but better — comfortably, safely, and independently in the place they love most: Home.

My focus on older adults in the home began as Executive Vice President of BrightStar Senior Care, where I saw firsthand how vital high-quality in-home medical and personal care is for individuals who require in-home assistance in later years of their lives.

My time as Chief Development Officer for FYZICAL Therapy & Balance Centers taught me the critical role that balance, strength, and mobility play in fall prevention — and how preventable so many devastating falls are.

41

Today, as President of TruBlue Home Service Ally, I lead a national organization dedicated to a single mission: helping older adults age in place successfully by creating safer living spaces and removing everyday risks.

Throughout this chapter, I want to give you more than a checklist — I want to share the lessons I've learned professionally and personally, so you can build a plan for your loved one that works not just today, but for years to come. Whether you're an adult child supporting aging parents, a medical professional advising patients, or both, my hope is that you come away feeling empowered and prepared.

Here's what I know for sure: *aging in place is a process*. When done right, it's safer, more affordable, and what older adults deserve, but it requires commitment, clear steps, and the willingness to think ahead.

To Build a Plan, Start with a Personal Why: Tragedy, Love, and a Lifelong Mission

In senior care, most leaders who have dedicated their careers and lives to the advancement of the industry have a profoundly personal story. Mine is no exception. And, my experience opened my eyes to how important it is to plan for the realities of aging and illness. The truth is that most falls and accidents are preventable. Most homes can be adapted. Most crises can be avoided — if families have the information and support to plan ahead.

Years ago, my mother's battle with cancer taught my family firsthand how hard it is to transform a home into a safe care space overnight. When her condition worsened, we moved her in with my sister so she could spend her final months surrounded by family. My sister and brother-in-law sacrificed so much — rearranging rooms, learning how to manage medications, coordinating with doctors and nurses. We did everything we could to keep her comfortable, but the emotional and physical strain on the family was immense.

As with many adults, my family's experience with caring for my mother was not the only time we were challenged, trying our best to take care of an aging parent.

One evening, my father-in-law, a strong, healthy man who prided himself on doing things himself, fell down the stairs in his own home and broke his neck. Although paramedics revived him, he was left paralyzed from the neck down. In that single moment, everything changed.

Suddenly, our family was plunged into a crisis no one was prepared for. We had to scramble to adapt a home that was never designed for the care of a quadriplegic. We began our research and started planning to rent a hospital bed, install ramps, and move furniture — but despite our best efforts, we were always a step behind. The house still had stairs, narrow hallways, and a bathroom that was far too small for the equipment he now needed.

For six months, we did everything possible to care for him, but complications set in. Ultimately, we lost him. He passed away surrounded by family, but also surrounded by heartbreak that, deep down, we all knew could have been prevented.

That tragedy left scars on our family, especially my children, who adored their grandfather. But it also gave me unshakable clarity about my life's purpose: To make sure other families don't have to learn these lessons the hard way and dedicate my career toward helping educate and build prevention opportunities through business.

This personal loss is why I pour my heart into my work at TruBlue Home Service Ally. It's why I speak so openly about the power of simple, proactive fall prevention — not just big renovations, but small everyday changes that can mean the difference between safety and tragedy.

I share my story because I want to help you find your why – whether it is to better prepare for your family's aging, your own aging or to help encourage you to make active changes, now. I also share my stories for those of you going through a tough time to let you to know that you are not alone.

The Three Principles of Aging in Place

When families think about helping a loved one age in place, they often picture big renovations — building ramps, widening doorways, maybe a complete bathroom remodel with a walk-in tub. In reality, aging in place is not just about the big change you make once — it's about ongoing upkeep of the home to ensure it remains safe as needs evolve.

After years of working with all types of professionals in this field, I've found that every successful plan for aging in place rests on three simple but powerful principles. Had I known what I know now, then, these three principles could have helped prevent some of the shortcomings of in-home care that we could offer to my mother and my father-in-law. When all three principles are in place, families worry less, loved ones stay safer, and emergencies are avoided more often. They are:

Principle #1: A Comprehensive Home Safety Assessment

Performing a home safety assessment is the foundation of creating a safe environment. Without it, you're guessing about what needs to be fixed. A proper assessment uncovers hidden hazards, identifies risky areas, and helps you prioritize changes based on real risk, not fear.

If there's one thing I wish every family understood, it's this: *most falls don't happen because there are age-associated declines in strength and balance, but rather due to a host of interacting factors that include the home not being designed to support their needs.*

A loose throw rug, a dark hallway, a single step that's just a little too steep — these hidden hazards are where most preventable falls begin. Yet many families don't see these dangers until it's too late. This is the reason a thorough home safety assessment is the first step in any aging-in-place plan.

<u>Why Assessments Matter</u>

- Falls send over 3 million older adults to emergency rooms each year.
- 1 in 4 older adults falls every year. A reminder of how common and serious fall risks can be
- Most of these falls happen at home.

The above aren't just statistics — they represent our parents, grandparents, and neighbors. And while medical care is critical after a fall, prevention is far better, less traumatic, and far less expensive than recovery.

A professional assessment reveals hidden dangers and gives families a clear, prioritized plan. It answers the question: *What needs to be fixed first to prevent an emergency tomorrow?*

<u>How to Get an Assessment</u>

There are two main approaches to getting an assessment:

A. Do-It-Yourself Walkthrough
Families can start with a simple inspection, inside and outside the home. Walk every room and entryway with fresh eyes. Look for:

- Uneven walkways
- Loose rugs or cords across walkways
- Door handles and locks – are they easy to open
- Dim or missing lightbulbs
- Steps without secure handrails
- Door thresholds that can be tripped over
- Bathroom floors that get slippery
- Furniture that blocks easy movement
- Check first-floor windows – are they easy to open in case of an emergency
- Write everything down. Take photos if needed. Fix what you can immediately — like swapping bulbs or removing tripping hazards.

B. Hire a Professional

A do-it-yourself check is a good start, but most families overlook subtle risks — especially if a loved one has mobility or vision changes. That's where experts come in. There are two main types:

Occupational Therapists (OTs) are trained to spot how an older adult's health and the home interact. They know what your parent might struggle with today — and what could become risky tomorrow.

Certified Aging-in-Place Specialists (CAPS) combine home remodeling knowledge with aging expertise to recommend practical, cost-effective fixes.

TruBlue Home Service Ally offers assessments too, with a focus on real-world solutions and clear action steps — plus the team to do the work properly and maintain it over time.

Tip:

In some states, Medicare Advantage plans or Medicaid waivers may cover part of an assessment and light home modifications if prescribed by a doctor or OT. Veterans Benefits can help too. Always ask — many families don't realize this help exists.

Principle #2: Meaningful Senior-Focused Modifications

Once you've completed a home safety assessment, the next step is to make changes that reduce risk immediately — and permanently. The good news? Many of the most effective modifications are simple, affordable, and can be done in an afternoon.

These aren't major remodels. We're talking about small, targeted upgrades that make everyday life safer, more accessible, and more comfortable — without making the home feel clinical or unfamiliar.

We once worked with a client named Evelyn, age 82, who had slipped twice in her bathroom within a year. Her daughter reached out in frustration, feeling overwhelmed by options. We assessed the home and made three key changes: installed grab bars, added a slip-resistant mat, and swapped the old bathroom bulb with a bright motion-sensor fixture.

Total cost: under $600. Result: Evelyn felt safer — and her daughter had peace of mind.

Families often worry about how to pay for modifications. Thankfully, there are more options than many people realize to perhaps cover costs:

• Medicare Advantage (in some states) covers light home modifications if recommended by a physician or occupational therapist.

• Medicaid Waivers in certain states provide funding for home adaptations.

• Veterans Benefits may cover larger modifications through grants like SAH (Specially Adapted Housing) or SHA (Special Home Adaptation).

- Local Aging Agencies often provide grants, discounts, or referrals to vetted professionals.

- Always ask. Even a short note from a doctor or OT can open the door to funding support.

After understanding how you can pay for the modifications, now you can start to identify high-impact, low-cost modifications:

- Grab Bars: Install them in bathrooms — especially by toilets and inside s howers or tubs. Today's designs are sleek and even double as towel holders, blending in with décor.

- Slip-Resistant Flooring: Add non-slip coatings or mats to tile and hardwood floors, especially in bathrooms, kitchens, and entryways.

- Lever-Style Door Handles: Replace round knobs with lever handles that are easier to open, especially for those with arthritis or reduced grip strength.

- Motion-Sensor Lighting: Place in hallways, bathrooms, stairwells, and bedrooms. This ensures older adults never need to fumble for switches in the dark.

- Tub Cuts and Walk-In Showers: A tub cut lowers the step-in height of a bathtub and can be installed quickly and affordably. For long-term needs, consider a curbless walk-in shower with seating and hand-held sprayers.

- Accessible Storage: Move frequently used items to waist level. Avoid the need for reaching, stretching, or climbing. Pull-out shelves are a great upgrade for kitchens and closets.

• Raised Toilet Seats and Comfort-Height Chairs: These make it easier and safer to sit and stand — reducing strain on knees and hips.

The right modification can extend your loved one's ability to live at home safely by years — and prevent the kind of fall that changes everything. You don't need a total remodel. You need the right plan, the right priorities, and a partner you trust to make it happen.

Principle #3: Consistent, Proactive Maintenance and Help with Daily Tasks

Many families do a fantastic job with the first two principles — they complete a thorough safety assessment and make smart modifications. But then they overlook what might be the most persistent risk: The everyday chores and small maintenance tasks that can tempt a senior into danger.

Even the safest house becomes dangerous if routine upkeep is ignored. A burnt-out hallway light, a loose stair tread, cluttered walkways, or a forgotten ladder can undo all your good work in an instant. Ongoing maintenance keeps a safe home safe.

When all three principles are in place, families worry less, loved ones stay safer, and emergencies are avoided more often.

Why does ongoing maintenance matter?

A safe home stays safe only if it's kept that way. Lightbulbs burn out. Smoke detectors need batteries. Weather and time wear down railings, steps, and walkways. A cracked driveway, a loose stair tread, or a leaking faucet left unchecked can all create hazards that can trip up even the most careful senior.

I always tell families: good maintenance is silent fall prevention. When the little things are handled, older adults never feel the need to risk their health doing them alone. Plus, routine home maintenance can prevent costly and/or major home repairs, saving money in the long run.

I once met a widower named George, age 79. He prided himself on being self-sufficient. One winter, he climbed a step ladder to change the battery in his smoke detector that was chirping — just like anyone would. He lost his balance, fell backward, and broke his hip.

That single fall led to three months in a rehabilitation facility, thousands in medical bills, and a permanent loss of mobility. Today, George can't climb stairs like he used to. A simple maintenance plan — or just asking for help — could have prevented that life-changing moment.

Here's how to make sure routine upkeep doesn't become a hidden threat:

Remove the temptation
Take away ladders and step stools altogether. If they're not in the house, your loved one won't be tempted to use them.

Create a simple repair log
Keep a notebook in the kitchen or by the phone. Encourage your loved one to jot down anything they notice — a flickering light, a squeaky door, a dripping faucet. Family or a trusted service can review and handle the list regularly.

Plan ahead for seasonal chores
Set clear dates for holiday decorating, gutter cleaning, snow shoveling, or yard work. If family can't cover everything, hire trustworthy help. Knowing someone will handle these tasks reduces the urge for older adults to "just do it themselves."

Consider a professional maintenance plan
At TruBlue Home Service Ally, for example, we offer monthly and seasonal maintenance subscriptions designed specifically for older adults. We do routine maintenance, handle repairs, and tackle to-do lists — giving families peace of mind that small problems won't turn into big accidents.

Fall prevention isn't only about what you change in the house — it's also about what your loved one *doesn't* do in that house. Remove hazards, but also remove the impulse to tackle risky tasks alone. Routine maintenance keeps your loved one safe and keeps your family's worry at bay.

Now that you understand the three principles, you can begin the process of communicating solutions with your loved ones – which is often a tough conversation, as none of our parents want to acknowledge aging and changing.

Step 1: Have an Open Conversation
Before you fix anything, talk with your loved one. Many older adults fear losing control, so be gentle. Pride can also be a big deterrent. Mention that the goal is a safer home for everyone, not just them, but safety for their friends and loved ones. Focus on their goals — staying safe and staying home.

Ask:
• Do you feel safe moving around the house, especially at night?
• Are there any spots you avoid because you feel unsteady?
• Do you have trouble with certain chores or reaching things?
• Listen with compassion, not judgment.

Step 2: Do a Walkthrough Together
Print a simple checklist using this chapter as your guide. Walk room by room together during the daytime and also at night when the lighting is different. Take note of the following:

- Tripping hazards (rugs, cords)
- Dark areas that need better lighting
- Loose handrails or steps
- High shelves with daily items

Tackle quick fixes immediately: replace bulbs, remove rugs, tidy clutter.

Step 3: Book a Professional Assessment
If your loved one has fallen before, has poor vision, or struggles with mobility, don't wait — get a pro's eyes on the home. Contact:

- A local Occupational Therapist (OT)
- A Certified Aging-in-Place Specialist (CAPS)
- TruBlue Home Service Ally for an assessment plus a clear action plan
- Ask the assessor for a written list of recommended changes, organized by priority.

Step 4: Tackle High-Impact Modifications
Focus first on:
- Grab bars in the bathroom
- Motion-sensor lights in hallways and stairs
- Non-slip mats and floor coatings
- Lever door handles
- Tub cut or walk-in shower if needed
- Check with Medicare Advantage, Medicaid waivers, Veterans Benefits, or your local Area Agency on Aging for possible financial help. A simple doctor's note can open funding options!

Step 5: Plan for Ongoing Maintenance
Make a written plan:
- Who checks for burned-out bulbs and loose railings each month?
- Who handles yard work and seasonal chores?

- Who decorates for holidays?
- Where will your loved one write down small issues?

If family can't cover everything, hire a reputable senior-focused provider like TruBlue Home Service Ally. A modest subscription saves thousands in emergency bills and, more importantly, prevents heartache.

Step 6: Consider Smart Tech
Start simple:
- A smart speaker for voice-controlled lights and reminders.
- A radar-based fall detector in the bathroom or bedroom.
- A video doorbell and smart lock for security and peace of mind.

Explain how each device works — older adults embrace tech when they see how it protects freedom.

The Future of Fall Prevention and Senior Home Safety

We've covered the basics: assess the home, make smart modifications, and plan for routine maintenance. But there's a powerful new layer that's making aging in place safer and more realistic than ever: technology.

The best part? Today's smart solutions respect privacy and independence — two things every older adult values deeply.

Non-Camera Fall Detection
One of the most exciting advances is non-camera fall detection. Traditional medical alert buttons rely on the person wearing them and pressing them — but what if they forget? Or can't reach it after a fall?

Modern radar-based or radio frequency (RF) sensors detect sudden, unusual motion — like a fall — without the need for cameras in private areas. If a fall happens, an alert is automatically sent to family, caregivers, or emergency services.

No cameras. No wearable devices. Just quiet, invisible protection.

One TruBlue Home Service Ally client, Ruth, lives alone but uses this type of system in her bathroom — the highest-risk area for falls. When she slipped on a wet floor, the system detected her fall immediately and alerted her daughter and 911. Ruth was found within minutes — frightened but okay. That system gave her family precious peace of mind.

Smart Home Assistants
Devices like Amazon Alexa or Google Nest do more than play music — they make daily life safer:

• Turn lights on and off by voice.
• Remind individuals to take medications.
• Call family or emergency contacts with a simple voice command.
• Control thermostats to maintain a safe home temperature.
• Simple voice control reduces the need to walk in the dark or fiddle with switches.

Smart Locks and Video Doorbells
Safety at the front door is often overlooked. Smart locks allow trusted family or caregivers to unlock the door remotely if help is needed. Video doorbells help older adults see who's there without needing to answer — or opening the door to strangers.

Bathroom Innovations
Bathrooms remain the number one fall zone. New products make them safer and more comfortable:

- Anti-scald faucets automatically regulate water temperature.
- Slip-resistant floor treatments can be professionally applied to existing tiles.
- Walk-in tubs and showers with built-in seating and hand-held shower heads make bathing safer and easier.

These upgrades don't just prevent falls — they reduce daily strain and boost confidence.

Technology + Human Care: A Winning Combo

I always remind families: technology is not a replacement for people. It works best when combined with human touch — routine family check-ins, professional maintenance visits, and genuine connection.

When smart devices and human care work together, they create an invisible safety net that supports an individual's freedom without sacrificing privacy or dignity.

My Final Thoughts: Aging in Place is a Promise — Not a Gamble

If there's one truth I've learned — as a business professional, son, husband, and father — it's this: Safe aging in place does not happen by accident. It happens because people take action.

My father-in-law's fall was not fate. It was preventable. A low handrail on only one side of the stairs, poor lighting, and a hard-to-find light switch — each was a small risk on its own. Together, they became the moment that changed his life and ours forever.

I share this not for sympathy, but as a call to every family.

Don't wait for a fall to decide your loved one needs help. Don't assume "it'll never happen to us." The reality is, falls are the leading cause of injury-related death for older adults — but they don't have to be.

When you build a plan based on the three principles — a solid safety assessment, practical modifications, and consistent, proactive maintenance — you create a living shield of protection around your loved one. When you add thoughtful technology and regular check-ins, you build a safety net that's stronger than any grab bar alone.

Most importantly, you give your parents, grandparents, or patients the greatest gift: the dignity to stay where they want to — surrounded by memories, family photos, the garden they love, and the neighbors they know.

At TruBlue Home Service Ally, we carry this mission in every home we visit. It's why we say every day: "Aging in place starts with the home™."

But it continues with you — the adult child, the caregiver, the nurse, the therapist, the trusted friend — who cares enough to plan ahead, ask hard questions, and tackle the small fixes before they become emergencies.

From my family to yours: thank you for caring enough to take action. Together, we can make aging in place not just possible, but safe, joyful, and full of the dignity every aging adult deserves.

[4]
The Caregiver's Advantage: Ageism Awareness

by
Eve Hill

What messages about aging have shaped your expectations of your loved one, or of yourself?

My grandmother had been strong and independent before ALS, but when the disease progressed and she could no longer walk, she refused to leave the house. She said she didn't want to be "pitied." My mother tried valiantly to coax her out. She even bought a van

> **Ageism:**
> Stereotypes (how we think)
> Prejudice (how we feel) and
> Discrimination (how we act)
> towards others or ourselves
> based on age.
> – *World Health Organization*

with a wheelchair lift. "You can do what you like with the van," said Grandma, "but I'm never going to ride in it."

The shame my grandmother felt was self-directed ageism. I was a kid back then and didn't have the word for it yet, or the awareness to offer an alternate narrative, but I saw how it shaped her experience, physically and emotionally. Her identity, her relationships, and her access to the world all shrank because of the stigma she associated with needing a wheelchair.

Today I'm a Certified Aging-in-Place Specialist, pro-aging strategist, and accessible design advocate. I can point to the research that supports what

I witnessed as a child: older adults who internalize negative age stereotypes show faster rates of functional decline and are less likely to seek preventive care. And I can offer strategies to recognize and combat the ageism you may encounter in caregiving, for positive impacts on the mental and physical health of all involved.

It's a tall order. Ageism is baked into our culture, our relationships, and our environments. It's pumped into "anti-aging" creams, stacked among the racks of "over the hill" birthday cards, built into home design features, classic fairy tales, current media, and public policy. Ageism is a manufactured barrier to aging with dignity and comfort. It can harm our health, and limit our choices and our sense of self-worth.

Why Ageism Awareness Matters in Caregiving

"Older adults who maintain positive age beliefs live an average of 7.5 years longer than those who don't."
-Dr. Rebecca Levy, Yale School of Public Health

Understanding how ageism influences care dynamics is the key to preserving the dignity and health of our loved ones. Our outlook on growing old can impact everything from memory and balance to recovery time, and even how long we live. Unexamined ageism in ourselves and our environments can create fear, false hope, resistance to care, and delay the practical decisions that prolong health and independence at home.

Caregivers who aren't aware of their ageist biases are more likely to base their expectations on assumptions rather than facts, dismiss legitimate medical concerns as "just part of aging," exclude older adults from their own care decisions, or jump into rescue mode and unintentionally undermine the independence of those in their care.

Caregivers who recognize and confront age-related biases provide measurably better care, build stronger bonds and mutual resilience. Think of your attitudes about aging as a direct line of support for you and your loved one. Your ageism awareness can become a source of strength for both of you.

Reframing Aging: The Positivity Effect

I think we can all agree that our society needs a more positive narrative for aging. The one we have now, where life is imagined as a steep arc that peaks in midlife, then plummets downward until the end, is outdated, discriminatory, and

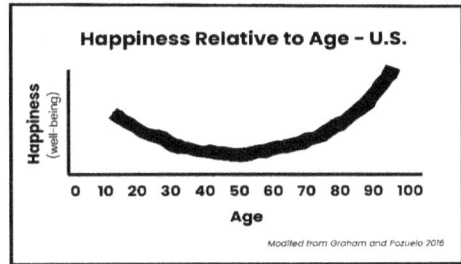

Happiness Relative to Age – U.S.

Modified from Graham and Pozuelo 2016

downright detached from reality. The truth is, age is no longer a reliable predictor of just about anything, including health. Personality, ambition, and self-determination are not dictated by age, and cognitive decline is not inevitable.

Research reveals a "U Curve" of Happiness to our life course, not an arc. We're happiest at the earlier and later stages of life.

Hang on! As my grandmother (and possibly yours) used to say, "Growing old isn't for sissies." Let's slap a reality check on all the bluebirds and rainbows, shall we? Okay. I'm not denying that aging into the longevity years can be hard. There are physical challenges, the loss of friends, facing mortality, and more. But ageist assumptions and negative age stereotypes make it worse. Growing old isn't easy, but maintaining the positive age beliefs that can add 7.5 years to our lives isn't as hard as you might think. That's because it's in our nature.

"Older adults pay attention to and remember more positive than negative information."
– Dr. Laura Carstensen, Stanford Center on Longevity

Give yourself permission to recognize the Assets of Maturity, like innovative thinking, resilience, problem-solving and tolerance for ambiguity. Consider gerontologists like Dr. James E. Birren, who saw advancing age not as a falling away of youth, but as progress toward a higher self, and Dr. Louise Aronson, who presents Elderhood as its own stage of development, with its own potential for growth and continued contribution to the social good.

We can push back against ageism by refusing to let the toughest parts of growing old define the whole. We can acknowledge the real challenges, while making space for the pro-aging and positive emotion strategies that erode ageism's negative impact on aging and caregiving relationships.

Strategies for Non-Ageist Communication

1. Attention on: Education
"Don't bounce back. Adapt forward."
– Anna Hall, Chief Culture and Community Officer, Front Porch Communities, at the LeadingAge Virginia Annual Conference 2025

Meet Donna. She's been a professional caregiver for over a dozen years. She speaks confidently about her work with the residents of a local continuing care community and her ability to encourage even the most reluctant among them to come out of their rooms for meals and activities. Even those living with advanced dementia, like a woman who had been spending her days in bed weeping, waking up each morning to the heartbreak of asking for a beloved husband who had died months before. There are still no easy answers, but with Donna on the scene, her days have taken a more active shape.

What's Donna's secret? A compassionate heart and hard work aren't enough. If they were, almost every family caregiver would have a smoother road. Donna didn't show up with the profound depth of personal relationship a spouse, partner or adult child brings to the table, but she's not nearly as susceptible to the layers of guilt, frustration, sadness, and sense of being overwhelmed that often come with caring for a member of one's own family.

Donna reports for duty with a professional toolkit, not emotional baggage. She also participates in regular training, including empathy education. A recent seminar had her wearing special eyewear to experience how a person with macular degeneration sees the world, and slipping on shoes with spikes inside to mimic neuropathy. "They don't feel like we do," she learned. "They see differently, they hear differently."

Most family caregivers have no such instruction. We grieve while we care, trying to hold on to who someone was. Donna doesn't carry that burden of reversal, but family caregivers sometimes learn on the fly how to let go of an impossible dream.

It's a remarkably contradictory experience. An aging parent or lifelong partner who personified wisdom or strength turns vulnerable and needs protection. Before a diagnosis of dementia, my father was a philosophy professor. An author, a teacher, and a thinker. But in the last year of his life, the people around him and the rooms in his own home became increasingly unfamiliar to him. These conflicting realities not only heightened my personal anguish, but also, as research suggests, my susceptibility to ageist attitudes. In times of emotional stress, our brains are more likely to rely on mental shortcuts, such as unconscious bias and societal stereotypes.

"I call it self-sabotage," says Consuela Marshall, Caregiver Coach. "They [family caregivers] may have a preconceived way of thinking that really clouds their ability to stay in the moment. It clouds the ability to separate from some things in the past and really see their loved one for what they can do now."

It may start with a little elderspeak, a common example of ageism. When caregivers harbor unconscious age-related biases, they might inadvertently infantilize older adults in their care, making assumptions about capabilities and desires, speaking in the high-pitched, sing-song tone routinely used with children.

Language and vocabulary have an impact on our perceptions and even on our health. However well intentioned, adopting a patronizing or exaggerated tone based on a person's age is a form of "othering," a manufactured barrier, not just between the older person and us, but between our present and future selves. And being on the receiving end of elderspeak? It's confusing when a word is exaggerated. It's more difficult to understand a statement that sounds like a question.

Elderspeak can decrease comprehension and undermine a person's trust in the speaker, cause them to lose confidence in their own decision-making, lower their self-esteem, and even lead to withdrawal or depression.

Simple communication shifts

Avoid Elderspeak:
Address older adults by their preferred names: Avoid diminutives like "sweetie" or "dear."

Instead of elderspeak: *"Are we ready for our medicine?"*
Use respectful adult dialogue: *"Would you like to take your medication now?"*

Instead of ordering: *"Time for your walk."*
Offer choice: *"Do you want to walk with me to the store?"*

Instead of directing: *"You should do it like this."*
Offer control: *"Would this be easier for you?"*

Instead of othering: *"What older people need is..."*
Offer inclusion: *"What we need when we're older is..."*

Observe/Listen/Reframe:
Is the behavior "resistance?" It could be hurt feelings, fatigue, fear, sensory overload, or simply a rejection of being treated as frail or incompetent.

2. Attention on: Agency

Who decides which actions to celebrate and which to dismiss? Let it be you, not ageism.

Benevolent Ageism

Caregivers, even with the best intentions, may accelerate dependence by taking over tasks their spouse, partner or parent might still manage. The practice is common enough to have a name, "Benevolent Ageism." It can also take the opposite form, like when we idealize our loved ones. Benevolent Ageism can lead to unrealistic care goals or misplaced pressure, inflating expectations beyond reason or pushing for medical miracles. Family caregivers often hold onto an image of who their loved one was, and anything less than 100% can feel like a total loss. Whether we rush in to do too much or hold on too tightly to who someone used to be, Benevolent Ageism blinds us to the here and now.

In my case, I carried the echoes of ageism from my grandmother's experience through the generations. Just a few years ago, my father came home from what would be his last hospital stay. His legs, already weak, had finally lost the strength to bear his weight. He couldn't get himself out of bed, and I couldn't accept it. I spun into "fix-it" mode, shifting from relating to rescuing, chasing an emotional wish for recovery. I fought for therapies that might make my father's desire to walk again come true, but it never did.

I realize now that my zeal was, in part, an attempted redemption of what happened with my grandmother, who wouldn't leave the house after she couldn't walk. I had thought my efforts were in line with my father's wishes, but in hindsight it looks more like a rescue mission that failed in the face of reality, straining relationships and causing distress and false hope in the person I was most trying to help. A benevolent kind of ageism was directing my family relationships and care decisions.

> *"It's a different kind of independence they're capable of, and they need to be given the space to figure that out."*
> – Consuela Marshall

We can adapt to the in-between, but it's not easy. Ageism obscures the subtle, embodied signals of agency, like a look, a gesture, or a choice, and carries the threat of reduced memory, lower recovery from illness, and even shorter life expectancy.

The Subtle Art of Agency

> *"And that's when I saw it. What it really means to age. What it means to live with stage six Alzheimer's. How meaningful it is to be next to someone during those moments."*
> - Danniel Fuchs, author, *The Ultimate Guide to Multigenerational Living*

We do have the power to recognize and uphold our loved one's personhood. Take the time to offer choice or inclusion, to notice a pattern, a gesture, or a moment of presence. I almost missed it, but one of the last memories I have of my father was the day I embraced that subtle definition of "agency," and his wordless glance showed me that not all change is disappearance, and not every loss erases what matters.

By then my father had difficulty swallowing. He couldn't walk and he could barely talk. His hearing aids were minimally effective. Stopping by his house before hitting the road back home, I left my backpack and a brown bakery bag in the doorway and went to his bedside to greet him.

My father's live-in caregiver was gifted at keeping up a steady chatter with him, but for me, the mixture of his physical limitations and the emotional wrenching of seeing my once all-powerful father approach the end made it difficult for me. Everything I came up with felt irrelevant, and yet I couldn't just sit there. Maybe I started describing a character I saw on the bus coming over, or something I was studying for the real estate exam at the time. I had slipped into the rescue mindset again, thinking I had to entertain him, "fix" the silence, so I almost missed the moment.

He didn't seem to be paying attention to me, which wasn't unusual, but what was unusual was the effort he was putting into looking past me. He was trying to speak but was frustrated. Eventually I saw he was working to bring one arm up from under the covers. I untucked the side of the sheet and he raised his arm, the watch he continued to wear (despite all his weight loss) dangling loosely off the end of his wrist. He pointed behind me, and said, "Bag."

The bakery bag! He didn't need my small talk, and he didn't need rescuing. My father wanted a scone. "Cherry cornbread scones," I said. An eyebrow raised and a small smile curled his lips, then mine. It felt good to have what he would have called a "gentle purpose."

So, I took my time. Removed all the dried cherries, mashed a bit of scone in a small bowl and poured in a lot of Ensure so it'd be smooth enough for him to swallow. When I came back in from the kitchen his caregiver was already there. I knew she'd be watching, so again I took my time. I was sort of watching myself, too. Here I am, feeding my father. As I dipped the spoon in the mixture and started to lift it to his mouth, his caregiver expressed her oft-repeated mealtime reminder, "Chew and swallow, Jerry, chew and swallow."

All of a sudden, that precious bite could wait. My father paused, no longer looking at the spoon but into my eyes. Then he rolled his own, with a knowing jest that will always stay with me. He wasn't agitated. He wasn't confused. It was his classic, familial eye roll. The one that said: "Can you believe this?" That was a moment when safety, procedure, and recognition all came together for me. When my father revealed himself, I was present.

Agency Action Steps
Ageism awareness helps caregivers shift perception. By detaching your loved one's behavior from ageist associations, it's possible to pick up on the feelings behind the words. To see the subtle, non-verbal cues that indicate preferences, discomfort and presence, even when speech, mobility or cognitive ability fades.

Look for:
• Facial expressions: a smile, a frown, an eyebrow lift
• Body language: reaching, recoiling, leaning in
• Responses or engagement with specific people, objects, or routines
• Small but consistent preferences: a favorite seat, flavor, or time of day

Record:

• Keep an observation journal: track mood, energy, or reactions at different times of day

Observe/Listen/Reframe (Again):

• Is the behavior "resistance?" It could be hurt feelings, fatigue, fear, sensory overload, or simply a rejection of being treated as frail or incompetent

3. Attention on: Environment

How much of our perception of health is shaped by the home itself?

"Older adults are unnecessarily disabled by standard design features."
- Esther Greenhouse, Longevity Strategist

Ageism-Proof Your Home
The way our society looks at aging has shaped the way we've built for it, and a lot of what we perceive as personal infirmity, resistance, or agitation has more to do with the design of the home than it does with the condition of the person. Stairs-only access, doorways too narrow for a walker or wheelchair, bathrooms lacking grab bars, rooms with poor lighting, doors too heavy to open, and high counters and cabinets are all outdated, manufactured barriers that unnecessarily disable older adults and undermine their independence.

"Decline Design" limits function and makes people feel incapable, even when they're not. It also distorts how others perceive our health. A low toilet or a hard-to-reach cabinet can suggest more frailty than actually exists. This is how home design becomes a carrier of ageism, and why home modifications for aging in place aren't just fall prevention; they're ageism prevention, influencing how we respond, how we provide care, and what we believe is possible.

A lack of understanding of options and aesthetics contributes to the stigma of home modifications, and in turn to deferred maintenance, to older adults "making do" in unsafe living conditions: using stepladders, navigating dark rooms, and self-limiting their use of spaces in their own homes.

In my father's case, ageism in his home design cost him comfort, dignity, and put him at higher risk for a fall. Once he needed a walker, his bathroom doorway was too narrow for him to enter. He had to make his way down the hall and down the stairs to take a shower. When I suggested modifications, he resisted. He said he wasn't "ready." Conditioning and pride pushed back against practical matters. Both that narrow doorway and that resistance was ageism in action.

Leveraging Design

Unconscious biases arising from Decline Design are neutralized by implementing principles that support mobility, autonomy, and longevity. Call it by any name you like: Universal Design, Accessible Design, Better Living Design, Visitable Design, Enabling Design, Lifespan Design. It's about building and remodeling homes that adapt to us as our needs change, reducing and even eliminating the need to adjust ourselves to our environment. Universal Design features include lever handles, touch faucets, curb-less showers, zero-step entrances, wide doorways, open floor plans and smart technology.

> **UNIVERSAL DESIGN:** "Universal Design is design that is usable by all people, to the greatest extent possible, without the need for adaptation or specialized design."
> –*Ron Mace, Center for Universal Design*

We can preserve dignity, prevent falls, save lives, reduce medical costs and stay longer in the homes we love by incorporating practical and stylish improvements before the need arises. Our homes can be welcoming not only to our future selves, but to everyone.

Theory of Relational Ageism

The Theory of Relational Ageism is just that: ageism perpetuating itself between people and rippling through families, generations, and professional considerations. At a recent presentation from a major 55+ living building company, the head of sales and marketing touted "10

Timely and Lasting Features" included in every new home build, like wider doorways, zero entry showers and wood blocking in the walls for grab bars... but not the grab bars themselves!

Because of the social stigma, some professionals still keep certain accessibility options hidden, as if safety is something to be ashamed of. That perpetuates the ageist messaging that has conditioned us to think these changes are ugly, or a symbol of personal shifts in abilities. It's human nature to try to hide what we perceive to be our weakness. That's why it's so important to change the way we look at home modifications.

Please don't fear the stigma. Decline Design elements are physically dangerous and emotionally diminishing. Accessible homes are a positive response to an ageist environment, preventing falls, saving on medical costs, offering elegant options, and meeting the needs of all ages and abilities.

> **Home Mod Heroics: Grab Bars**
>
> Sleek and stylish grab bar designs are available in all the colors of the rainbow. Choose from fancy finishes, like a wood grain look, or have them customized with your favorite team logo. "Optimized" grab bars double as medicine cabinets, soap dishes, and toilet roll holders. There are textured grab bars, grab bars inlaid with tile to match your shower, grab bars that curve around corners, stretch from floor to ceiling, and fold up and down out of walls.

What are we waiting for?

75% of older adults want to age in place
10% of U.S. homes are ready to age with us
At some point most of us will face the decision: Modify or Move?

Take a look at your caregiving environment. What does it assume about aging? Does it offer inclusive features that support the dignity of older adults and allow them to see themselves in a positive future, or do its design features create ageist obstacles?

When we realize the limitations and risks we've been living with are due to ageism and not just aging, we're more likely to make the changes that will prolong independence at home.

Who benefits from an Ageism-Proof home?

Basically everyone.

Home environments unsuitable for aging in place increase physical strain, risk of injury and contribute to caregiver burnout. Ageism-proof homes prevent a majority of falls, support independence, promote well-being, and repair our nation's housing infrastructure. Combating ageism in home design and embracing home modifications as safe and stylish lifestyle upgrades means fewer falls and hospitalizations, and up to 42% fewer caregiver hours. Grab bars, ramps, and other practical and stylish home modifications mean your loved one can lean on them for physical support, not you.

Action Steps: Reframing Home Mods

Home modifications offer solutions to problems our loved ones may not yet feel they need to address, but the risks of inaction are too big to ignore. A few simple, thoughtful changes in the home can prevent falls, support autonomy, and send an age-friendly message that allows your loved one to imagine themselves in a positive future.

Avoid:

The "problem frame," which presents accessibility and aging as something to fix instead of support.

Instead of: *"You need to install grab bars because you're old and might fall."*

Say: *"These grab bars will make moving around our home easier for everyone."*

Emphasize:

Aspirations, not fears.

• Creature comforts and emotional rewards. Improved quality of life, not just safety.

• Enhancing convenience, autonomy and allowing more time with family.

• Providing spaces that adapt over time.

Talk and Listen:

• Plan modifications together. It reinforces agency, and they may even get excited about the options, starting with the color of the grab bars!

• Be willing to try new approaches.

What if Nothing Changes? Skepticism and Solutions

"I'm not afraid of doing hard things, but I'm worried about the future."
- Angela B., family caregiver

Maybe you're thinking, thanks for the advice, but my loved one is still not making positive choices or taking care of themselves. There's healthy food in the refrigerator, I've organized the medications, set up the power of attorney. I'm managing their household, their chronic illnesses, but how do I deal with my own fear that it's not going to get any easier?

The Shift is in Us

"Overcoming denial is your first step."
- C.A.L.M. (Caregivers Are Learning More), USC Family Caregiver
Resource Center

Ageism Awareness in caregiving isn't about fixing someone or erasing a lifetime of cultural messaging about aging. As caregivers, we inherit and project ageist messages, too. Especially when the dynamics flip and we start doing for our loved ones the things they once did for us.

Ageism Awareness in caregiving is a tool to recognize your own patterns, your own assumptions. As acknowledged in the book *You and Your Aging Parent*, this kind of detached calmness can be a Herculean effort, but it's better than trying to order or argue. Positive emotion strategies, empathy education, and paying attention to agency and environment are tools for grounding yourself and protecting your connection to your loved one.

My mother, now approaching her 90th birthday, describes caring for my grandmother as a "privilege." "Yes, it was difficult," she says. "Very difficult. ALS is heartbreaking. But the months of intimacy we had were infinitely valuable and remain a deeply treasured memory."

Ageism Awareness Works

Fighting ageism means working both externally, like modifying homes, and internally, like confronting our core beliefs about aging and the fears that come with seeing our parents or partners age.

Good News: Even one-time Ageism Awareness interventions (like reading this chapter!) can help people shift perspectives for the long term. Study follow-ups have shown that, even after just one workshop, participants continue to avoid making assumptions about older people and use language with them that respects autonomy.

Improving communication, repairing relationships and bettering health outcomes are all fueled by ageism awareness. Notice how it helps you adjust how you speak, recognize a moment of agency, or make the space more accessible. Caregiving will change you, and ageism awareness will change how you care.

[5]
Technology Supported Caregiving for Aging in Place

By
Dr. Julie A. Brown and Dr. Jocelyn Brown

Gloria's Story

Gloria is 78 years old and lives alone in the same home she and her husband bought nearly forty years ago. Since her husband's passing, Gloria has worked to maintain her independence. She still cooks for herself, enjoys short walks when her knees allow, and cares for her small dog, Max, who provides daily companionship and comfort. Max is a bundle of energy and tends to circle her legs when he's excited, especially during walks around the block. Gloria has rheumatoid arthritis, which makes bending, twisting, and standing for long periods difficult. She has noticed more stiffness in her joints lately and sometimes struggles to manage tasks like carrying laundry up and down the steps or leaning down to open the dishwasher.

Gloria's daughter, Liana, lives two towns away and visits every weekend. During the week, she calls daily and helps with tasks like scheduling appointments and paying bills. While Gloria enjoys their talks, she misses the social interaction she once had through community events, weekly church groups, and regular outings with her husband. Her world has grown quieter, and the emotional weight of that change is beginning to settle in. She has started to feel less motivated to stick with her usual routine. Occasionally, she forgets small things, like where she placed the remote or whether she already fed Max. These moments frustrate her and sometimes make her question her memory.

Liana tries to keep track of everything, but she feels stretched thin. She often calls during her lunch break, hoping Gloria answers. When she doesn't, Liana wonders if something has happened or if her mom is just resting. She's begun to feel a quiet worry in the back of her mind that is always there. Although Gloria wants to remain in her home and care for Max, even she has started to wonder how long that will be possible.

Neither Gloria nor Liana has explored caregiving technology. They use basic cell phones and feel unsure about adding new devices. Gloria worries about the cost of new gadgets while Liana feels overwhelmed by the number of options. For now, they rely on handwritten notes, regular phone calls, and their shared hope that things will stay manageable.

Reflection Questions

1. What caregiving challenges stood out to you in Gloria's story?
2. How might these situations create stress or uncertainty for both Gloria and her daughter?

Can you think of one or two technology devices that could support this caregiving situation?

Introduction

Caregiving today looks different from what it did a generation ago. It's also important to recognize that many older adults live independently without needing caregiving. However, the chance of needing assistance increases with age as health issues, mobility challenges, or memory concerns start to impact daily routines. While the core values of love, support, and protection stay the same, the tools available to caregivers are rapidly evolving. As more older adults prefer to age in place, family members and support providers are turning to technology to bridge the gaps, especially when distance, time, or energy make hands-on daily care difficult.

This chapter encourages readers to think about how technology can aid the caregiving process. Whether you are a spouse, sibling, neighbor, or adult child, you might discover that technology provides new ways to help, monitor, and stay connected with the older adult in your life. Selecting the right tools requires careful planning, clear communication, and continuous adjustment.

The goal of this chapter is to guide how to integrate technology into caregiving for aging in place smartly. This refers to the ability of older adults to remain in their own homes and communities safely, independently, and comfortably for as long as possible. We will begin by reviewing the range of caregiving technologies that are currently available, from simple, low-tech tools to advanced systems that rely on Wi-Fi or smart platforms. From there, we will explore how to select, adapt, and use these tools in ways that prioritize the needs and comfort of the older adult. Throughout, we will keep the human side of caregiving at the center.

Categories of Caregiving Technology for Aging in Place

Technologies that support caregiving in the home come in many forms. They range from familiar household tools to complex devices that require internet access and remote management. These tools can assist with safety, communication, health management, socialization, mobility, and daily routines. Below is a general overview of these categories, with examples.

Low-Tech Solutions
Low-tech tools are often the most accessible. They are typically inexpensive, easy to use, and do not require internet access. Many caregivers begin with these options.

- **Medication organizers:** Pillboxes labeled by day or time of day help older adults manage medications.

- **Grab bars and non-slip mats:** These basic safety tools reduce the risk of falls in bathrooms and hallways.

- **Light timers or motion-activated night lights:** These improve nighttime visibility and can prevent disorientation.

Mid-Tech Solutions

These tools offer more features and may include simple digital elements. They may require occasional setup but are generally user-friendly.

- **Amplified phones:** Telephones with adjustable volume and larger buttons for easier calling.

- **Medical alert buttons:** Wearable devices that connect the user to emergency services when pressed.

- **Digital photo frames with messaging features:** These allow families to send updated pictures or notes, offering connection and emotional support without the need for smartphones or apps.

The devices above can have more advanced options, such as a display screen to show a live transcript of a phone call or a medical alert feature on a smart watch. When these options are available or are featured on devices, it involves a greater level of technology and is then categorized as "high tech," as described in the section below.

Smart Home Devices

High-tech solutions often require Wi-Fi, smartphone access, or cloud-based systems. They can offer advanced features such as automation, remote monitoring, and real-time alerts. These tools are especially useful when caregivers live at a distance or when older adults want more control over their daily routines.

- **Voice assistants (e.g., Alexa, Google Nest):** These respond to voice commands and can provide reminders, play music, and control other smart devices.

- **Home sensors:** Motion detectors or door sensors can send alerts to caregivers if routines change.

- **Pressure mats:** Placed beside a bed or in doorways, these mats send alerts when stepped on, helping caregivers monitor movement and be aware of wandering or nighttime falls.

- **Smart kitchen appliances:** Kitchen devices, such as some modern stoves, ovens, and coffee makers, can be controlled remotely or programmed with timers and sensors via an app. These can reduce the risk of accidents and help older adults manage cooking tasks more safely.

Each of these tools can be helpful, but success depends on how they are selected, introduced, and used. The next section explores how caregivers can make smart choices when bringing technology into the caregiving environment.

Smart Integration: How to Thoughtfully Add Technology to Your Caregiving Plan

Keeping Humans at the Center

Technology works best in caregiving when it complements, *not replaces*, human care. Tools should enhance connection, provide support, and reduce stress, not create new barriers or frustrations. As with any caregiving decision, the person receiving care must remain central in the planning and decision-making process.

Caregivers should think of technology as a support beam rather than the entire structure. When thoughtfully integrated, it can provide reassurance, improve safety, and give caregivers more time and flexibility. But if introduced too quickly (if the adult is unfamiliar with the technology) or without considering the older adult's preferences and comfort, even the best tool can fall flat.

Starting Small

A smart caregiving plan that involves integrating technology often begins with just one or two small changes. Rather than outfitting a home with every available tool, it is often more effective to choose a single device that addresses a clear need. For example, if missed medications are a concern, a simple talking reminder or smart pill organizer might be a good place to start. If safety at night is the issue, motion-activated lights or a bedside pressure mat can provide reassurance.

It is important to consider who will set up the device and who will troubleshoot if something goes wrong. Choosing user-friendly tools, ideally ones that both the caregiver and the older adult can learn together, can ease the learning curve. Products that offer phone-based support or how-to videos are often more successful over time.

It also helps to choose devices that are minimally disruptive to routines. For example, a voice assistant that gives gentle reminders during the day may be less intrusive than wearable devices that must be charged, worn, or checked regularly. Respect for the older adult's space and lifestyle is essential.

Tailoring Tech to the Person

Not every older adult wants or needs the same kind of support. Some embrace new technology with enthusiasm, while others approach with caution or resistance. Caregivers should match the product to the older adult's strengths, experience with technology, and comfort level. This might involve choosing devices with larger and brighter screens, clear audio, or fewer steps for interaction.

For example, an older adult with hearing challenges might benefit from an amplified phone or a video calling device with captioning. Someone with mild memory loss might respond well to visual reminders, color-coded switches, or routine-based voice prompts. A person who loves music or storytelling may find connection through a voice assistant that plays their favorite albums or audiobooks.

Motivation plays a key role in whether these tools are accepted and used. Some older adults may be more willing to wear a device or use a platform if they see how it helps them stay independent and maintain autonomy. Others may feel motivated by the idea of staying socially connected or avoiding worry for a family member. These motivations should be explored and supported, since even the best-designed technology depends on active engagement.

Cultural preferences, language, personal history, and one's budget also play a role. The caregiving technology should feel familiar and respectful. If a device feels intrusive or patronizing, it is less likely to be welcomed. Listening to concerns and involving the older adult in selection can help create shared understanding and reduce tension.

Building Resilient Care Networks

Technology can be a strong thread in a wider caregiving net, but it should never be the only one. A successful aging-in-place plan often includes both digital tools and human connection. This might mean combining remote monitoring with regular check-in calls or using shared digital calendars to coordinate visits among family and neighbors.

Building this network takes time and communication. Caregivers should think about who else can be involved that would be welcomed by the adult: friends, extended family, neighbors, community volunteers, or professionals. Digital platforms can help connect these people, but the relationships themselves must be nurtured offline as well. For example, a family might use a shared app to manage tasks like grocery shopping, rides to appointments, or weekend visits. Meanwhile, a local church or community center might provide friendly callers or drop-in support. Together, this mix of personal and tech-based support creates a stronger, more adaptable caregiving plan.

In summary, the smartest tech solutions are not the ones with the most features, but those that fit best into a person's life. They respect dignity, encourage autonomy, and support caregivers without replacing them. By starting small, matching tools to people, and weaving tech into a broader care network, families can create systems that truly help older adults thrive at home.

Expanded Caregiving Technologies for Aging in Place

The devices below reflect just a small sampling of caregiving technology options. These devices endeavor to recognize the full humanity of older adults, addressing not only safety and medical concerns but also the need for joy, autonomy, creativity, and connection.

Table 1. Examples of caregiving technologies to support aging in place.

Device / Tool	What It Does	How It Helps the Older Adult	How It Helps the Caregiver	Price Range
Smartwatch with Fall Detection	Detects falls and sends alerts automatically	Offers discreet, wearable safety monitoring	Sends immediate alerts in emergencies	$150–$300+
Induction Cooktop	Only heats when the pan is present, surface stays cool	Safer cooking with a lower risk of burns	Reduces worry about kitchen fires	$60–$200+
Smart Water Leak Detector	Alerts when water leaks are detected	Prevents flooding and damage	Helps maintain a safe living environment	$30–$100
GPS Shoe Insoles	Tracks location discreetly via a shoe insert	Supports independence while addressing wandering	Can locate an older adult quickly if disoriented	$150–$300
Window or Cabinet Open Sensors	Sends alerts when windows or cabinets are opened	Can prevent wandering or unsafe food access	Adds a layer of safety without being intrusive	$20–$70 each
Wearable Air Quality Monitor	Measures indoor air (humidity, VOCs, CO2)	Promotes respiratory health	Alerts the caregiver to environmental risks	$100–$200
Smart Calendar Display	Shows a personalized daily schedule on a large screen	Helps with routine, reduces anxiety	Can update events or reminders remotely	$150–$250
App-Controlled Pet Feeder	Dispenses pet food at scheduled times	Keeps pets healthy and older adults on schedule	Removes the stress of pet care for caregivers	$70–$150
Two-Way Smart Intercom System	Easy room-to-room or house-to-house communication	Enables quick check-ins without a phone	Offers instant, hands-free updates	$60–$120 per set

Digital Jukebox or Music Table	Touchscreen music player with retro styling or sensory input	Sparks joy, memory, and relaxation	Promotes mood, reminiscence, and conversation	$200–$1,500
Virtual Reality (VR) Experience Kits	Offers immersive tours, games, or social meetups	Promotes fun, engagement, and reminiscence	Encourages cognitive stimulation, reduces isolation	$300–$800+
Digital Memory Book App or Device	Displays photos with captions and voice notes	Supports storytelling and identity	Encourages connection and conversation	$80–$200
Voice-Controlled Puzzle or Game Device	Allows play with trivia, games, or storytelling	Offers fun and cognitive engagement	Shared laughter, ease of interaction	$30–$90
Smart Picture Frame with Video Chat	Displays rotating photos and allows drop-in video calls	Ongoing connection with loved ones	Reduces feelings of isolation	$150–$250
Smart Oven with Auto Shut-Off	Automatically powers off after a set time or inactivity	Prevents overcooking or fire hazards	Reduces safety concerns around cooking	$300–$800+
Drawer-Style Dishwasher	Loads from waist height to avoid bending or tripping	Easier to use for those with limited mobility	Safer and simpler cleanup, less physical strain	$700–$1,200+

Tech Fatigue for Older Adults

For older adults, especially those managing physical limitations or emotional challenges such as grief or loneliness, technology can present barriers alongside benefits. Devices that are difficult to navigate, constantly send alerts, or require frequent updates can lead to frustration and disengagement.

• **Cognitive Load:** Learning how to use new tools can be mentally taxing, especially when instructions are unclear, or interfaces are cluttered.

• **Alert Overload:** Frequent reminders or prompts may be intended to help, but they can also become disruptive. Some older adults may begin to tune them out or feel anxious when they cannot respond quickly.

• **Loss of Autonomy:** Tools that track movement or behavior may feel intrusive, even when well-meaning. If an older adult feels watched instead of supported, trust in the tool and the caregiving relationship can erode.

Tech Burnout for Caregivers

Caregivers can also experience tech burnout. The same systems meant to reduce stress can increase it if they demand constant attention or technical troubleshooting.

• **Management Overload:** With each new device comes another app, password, interface, and set of updates to manage. The mental energy required to stay on top of it all can become overwhelming.

• **False Sense of Security:** When caregivers rely heavily on alerts and sensors, they may be caught off guard when devices malfunction or fail to report accurately.

• **Emotional Strain:** Monitoring someone you love through constant notifications can lead to hyper-vigilance and emotional exhaustion. It becomes difficult to relax when you are always on alert.

Human-Centered Strategies for Avoiding Tech Fatigue

To prevent technology from becoming a source of stress, caregivers and families can take the following steps:

- **Start Small:** Only introduce one tool at a time. Let it become part of the routine before adding another.

- **Choose Passive Support When Possible:** Devices like pressure mats or automated lights offer help without requiring interaction. These can be less disruptive for both the caregiver and the older adult.

- **Create Tech-Free Time:** Build in moments during the day where no devices are in use. Examples include mealtimes, walks, or quiet reflection.

- **Reassess Regularly:** A device that was useful last year may not be necessary today. Set a regular schedule, such as every 6 to 12 months, to evaluate which tools are still helpful and which may be adding unnecessary complexity.

- **Honor Preferences:** If an older adult strongly dislikes a device, that feedback matters. Find an alternative or adjust the settings to make it less intrusive.

Final Thoughts on Tech Fatigue and Burnout

Technology should support caregiving, not complicate it. When thoughtfully chosen and periodically reviewed, tools can enhance safety, autonomy, and peace of mind. However, when too many devices compete for attention or replace rather than complement human care, the result can be fatigue instead of relief.

Keeping the person at the center of caregiving means recognizing that rest, simplicity, and presence is just as valuable as innovation. A smart caregiving plan does not require every smart device. It requires intention, balance, and the willingness to pause when needed.

Shared Decision-Making: Introducing Technology Through Conversations

Technology should not be something that is *done to* an older adult. Instead, it should be something *explored with* them. At its best, caregiving technology becomes an extension of trust. In other words, a tool that supports both safety and dignity. But for that to happen, decisions about what to use, when to use it, and how to use it must be made together. One of the most respectful ways to bring technology into caregiving is to start with a conversation. Caregivers may feel tempted to rush in with new tools out of worry or urgency, but pausing to ask thoughtful questions first can make all the difference.

Before suggesting a device, it helps to ask:

1. What part of your day feels most frustrating or tiring?
2. What are examples of situations where you may wish someone could be there to help?
3. What would make your daily routine feel a little easier?
4. What might make your day more enjoyable?

These open-ended questions allow the older adult to reflect and share their own goals. For example, an older adult may express frustration over keeping track of appointments. This opens the door to suggesting a shared calendar display or a voice assistant that offers daily reminders. When the tool solves a problem the older adult identifies, it becomes a solution rather than an intrusion.

It can also help to offer choices. If a caregiver is hoping to introduce a safety tool, they might ask, "Would you feel more comfortable with something you wear, like a watch, or something we place in the room, like a motion light or sensor?" Involving the older adult in these decisions builds trust and makes success more likely.

Starting small also matters. A single, well-chosen device is often more helpful than a box of gadgets that never get used. Begin with one change, let it become part of the routine, and add new devices only as needed and wanted.

Privacy, Ethics, and Respect in Tech-Enabled Care

As technology becomes more involved in caregiving, it is important to stay grounded in ethics and respect. Monitoring tools, like cameras or motion sensors, can feel intrusive if not used thoughtfully. Even when caregivers are motivated by love or concern, devices that track movement, location, or behavior must be used with clear consent.

Older adults have the right to make decisions about their environment and their privacy. If a tool is going to collect data, send alerts, or be viewed remotely, it should be discussed in advance. Consent is not just a form to sign or an assumed understanding; it is an ongoing conversation. It is okay to revisit the conversation over time as needs and preferences evolve.

In some families, there may be tension about how much tech is "too much." For example, one sibling of an older adult might want to install cameras, while another worries about dignity and trust. These are not easy conversations, but they are important. Framing the conversation around values rather than tools can help: "We want to make sure Dad feels safe and connected. How do we do that in a way that also makes him feel respected and independent?"

Respect can also be shown through placement. A motion sensor at the front door may feel supportive, while a camera in the living room may feel invasive. Choose the least intrusive option that still provides the needed support. Always lean toward transparency and simplicity.

Revisiting Gloria's Story

Let us return to Gloria, who was managing loneliness, arthritis, mild memory concerns, and the daily demands of living alone.

Gloria's daughter, Liana, was beginning to feel overwhelmed, and both were unsure of how long Gloria could remain at home safely. After talking through some of their shared concerns, Liana and Gloria decided to explore a few simple technologies together. They started with a voice assistant that could help Gloria check the weather, play her favorite tunes, and set reminders. Gloria picked out a name for the assistant and enjoyed asking it for jokes each morning. They also added a smart pet feeder to keep Max on a feeding schedule.

A smart calendar display was placed in the kitchen to show upcoming appointments, medication times, and even pictures that Liana could upload remotely. This gave Gloria a sense of structure and connection. They added motion-activated lights in the hallway, which helped at night when Gloria got up to use the bathroom.

None of these changes happened overnight. They added one device, waited to see how it worked, and then talked about what felt helpful. Some ideas were paused or skipped. Gloria was always part of the decision, and Liana always asked how it made her feel.

Now, Gloria reports feeling more confident. She still has hard days, but the routine feels manageable again. Liana feels relief, knowing that support is present even when she cannot be there in person. The caregiving partnership remains rooted in love and is now supported by thoughtful technology.

This story is not about gadgets saving the day. It is about how small, intentional changes can make life more comfortable and relationships stronger. At its best, caregiving technology does not replace care. It enhances it.

Final Thoughts

Caregiving is one of the most personal and powerful roles a person can take on. Whether you are helping a parent, a partner, a friend, or a neighbor, the goal is often the same. You want to provide comfort, safety, and dignity while honoring the wishes of the person in your care.

Technology, when chosen thoughtfully and used with respect, can support that goal. It can extend independence, ease daily burdens, and create new ways to stay connected. But technology is not the main character in this story. The caregiver is. The older adult is. The relationship between them matters most. Every tool mentioned in this chapter, from a simple light timer to a voice-activated device, serves a larger purpose. These devices support human connection and promote independence. They strengthen caregiving relationships. They offer peace of mind.

As you explore the possibilities of caregiving technology, continue asking the questions that matter. What does the older adult want? What brings them joy? What feels comfortable, safe, and useful? Begin with one small step. Move at a pace that feels manageable. Keep your focus on what matters most. In the end, the best caregiving plan leads with compassion and grows through curiosity. Technology is not a replacement for care. It is a companion to it.

[6]

Why Bathroom Safety Matters for Older Adults – and Their Caregivers

By
Mark Conacher

I've worked within the bathroom industry in one way or another for nearly 40 years. Starting out in construction as a teenager, I've installed more bathrooms than I've had hot dinners, I founded an award-winning kitchen and bathroom installation business, and today, I am managing director of a patented anti-slip shower solution that is easy to clean, comfortable to stand on and most importantly, reduces the risk of slips in the shower to less than one in a million.

For many years I worked directly in people's homes, understanding the challenges they were facing with their existing bathrooms, and working out ways to make them better and safer. I think I've seen just about everything you can see in a bathroom, but one thing never changes. It's one of the most dangerous rooms in the home, and it doesn't matter whether you're young or old, frail or athletic; if a bathroom is unsafe, it's a problem waiting to happen - to you.

A big part of my work is about educating as many people as possible on the true cause of slips in the shower and what safety-focused solutions are out there. My focus is to help older adults, their families, and the caregivers

91

who support them, to understand the pros and cons of the different products available.

When people think about bathroom safety, they often picture grab bars and maybe a raised toilet seat. And while these are useful tools, they are just part of a bigger picture. Safety in the bathroom does not come from one single item. It comes from the way the space as a whole is designed. From what you stand on, to the lighting above your head.

This chapter isn't about selling any specific product, it's about keeping people who need a little help, safer. More than that, it's about easing the physical and emotional load on the individuals who care for them. If you've ever tried to help someone step in and out of a shower or support them while they use the toilet, you'll know it's not as easy as it sounds. One wrong step and someone's on the floor, and suddenly, everything changes.

Caregivers often carry a silent, but critical responsibility. This chapter is for them. I hope to give you practical advice, based on real experience. You don't have to be an expert in bathroom design to make good decisions. You just need honest information and the willingness to take safety seriously.

Understanding the Risks - It's More Than Just Slips

We should begin with the basics.
Most accidents in the bathroom come down to one thing: a loss of balance. And the place it happens most often? The shower.
You are barefoot in a wet, soapy environment; add in a split second of inattention.
Boom - You're on the floor. That's all it takes.

Now, while we usually associate these kinds of falls with older adults, that just isn't the case. Just this year (2025), Freddie Freeman of the LA

Dodgers, one of the top baseball players in the world, slipped in the shower and injured himself. He is a professional athlete who will have high-level strength and balance. If it can happen to him, it can happen to anyone.

Slips don't occur simply because of age or strength. They occur when contaminants like water, soap scum, shampoo or even your own body-oils comes between your foot and the surface of the shower or floor.

That's the science behind it, and this is why what you're standing on matters so much.

You can't stop a shower from getting wet, but you can control what the shower or floor is made of and how that material handles moisture.

Now, not all shower or floor surfaces are created equal. Some are sold as slip-resistant or anti-slip or even non-slip. What do these terms even mean? Ahh, the power of marketing.

Most people will believe they all mean the same thing, buy this and you won't slip. But that's not entirely true. There are subtle differences between the terms. Either the surface has been engineered to be anti-slip, something has been added to make it slip-resistant, or when two materials are brought together, they are naturally non-slip.

I will add that there is nothing non-slip about bare feet, water, soap or dirt, therefore this term should be eliminated completely for bathrooms.

Some surfaces rely on coatings that will at some point need reapplication and will lose their effectiveness after just a few years or even a few months. It really comes down to how often they are used and how well they are cleaned and maintained.

Applied coatings can be hard to keep clean and they can quickly degrade when common cleaners are used, or you start scrubbing at the surface to get it clean. This is where even a shower tray sold as slip-resistant can go wrong if you don't maintain it properly.

A surface that is unpredictable or can't easily be kept clean is a dangerous surface.

Before you choose a surface, learn as much as you can about the product:
• Ask about the slip test results.
• Ask how it stands up over time.
• Ask what cleaning products you can safely use.
• Ask if there's a coating and how often it needs to be reapplied.
• Ask if it will wear away if you scrub it?
• Ask what happens when soap scum builds up?
• Ask about the guarantees.

There are some excellent, permanent anti-slip solutions out there. Surfaces that don't rely on applied coatings and instead have an anti-slip texture manufactured into the tray during production. SENSTEC is a great example of this type of shower tray. The anti-slip is not painted on or added after the fact, it's part of the tray itself, and it doesn't wear off. SENSTEC is just one option for high-level safety, but it shows that smart design can lead to lasting protection from slipping.

If you're helping someone with bathing, whether once a day or once a week, this kind of stuff matters; it matters a lot. A slip in the shower doesn't just affect the person in the shower, it will affect you too. You're the one helping them back on their feet. You're the one dealing with the injury, the hospital, the doctors. A fall can derail everything.

It's also not just the physical risk; there's the emotional trauma too. Many caregivers feel guilty or helpless when someone falls. Left constantly asking themselves what they could have done differently. It may well be that there was nothing they could have done at that moment. But maybe that fall could've been avoided altogether with better planning or safer materials.

That's why this chapter will keep coming back to two key points:
• Safety isn't a luxury.
• Fit-for-purpose products, installed properly, can have a big impact.

It all comes down to recognizing a problem before it happens and making informed choices. The good news is, you are not alone and there are a lot of great businesses out there to help you do exactly that.

We can all agree that caring for someone in the bathroom is an extremely tough job, physically and emotionally, and no matter whether you're in there helping one of your parents, your partner, or if you are a professional helping a client, the bathroom can be a demanding place to provide care.

There's so little space to move around and you're often reaching and twisting at the same time as trying to hold on to someone. You're focused on keeping the individual safe, but you're also trying to avoid hurting yourself in the process. And as previously highlighted, this all usually takes place in a wet environment, in a space with very little room for error.

Then there's the emotional side - for both.

Other than when you were a young child, the bathroom is always a private place. Helping someone to wash, go to the toilet, or even just get ready for the day ahead can feel very uncomfortable for both of you. The person you're helping is guaranteed to feel embarrassed. You yourself might feel awkward, or unsure if you're doing it right.

For family caregivers, all of this can weigh heavily and start taking its toll. You're not just helping out; you're often making big sacrifices at the same to do it. There's a good chance you'll be juggling work and all your other family responsibilities, and let's not even talk about your own health. All this, while making sure someone else is safe and feels cared for.

Professional caregivers face a different kind of pressure. Often expected to be extremely efficient and, at the same time, be emotionally supportive, no matter what the day has thrown at them. You will be trying to maintain the person's dignity at all costs, all while working in a space that wasn't exactly designed with any level of caregiving in mind. But you still have to get the job done.

This is why bathroom design matters.

A well-thought-out bathroom won't just help the person being cared for, it will also ease the strain and the pressure on the person doing the caring. This can mean things like less lifting and fewer awkward positions. Overall, it can help give the carer more confidence.

When you remove the obstacles, everything becomes more manageable:
• There's no need to worry about slipping because the surface is clean and safe.
• There's no extra reaching because there are grab bars where they should be and will take the weight.
• There's no guessing if the person can manage alone, because they have the right products and support in place.

Getting the products and the design right will make a real difference. It will help protect you, your peace of mind, and your ability to care long term.

We should look for ways to make the bathroom safer, not just for those at risk, but for those who stand alongside and help them every day.

Inside the Shower

As we know, the shower is the riskiest place in the bathroom. Water, shampoo, soap, bare feet. From a safety standpoint, it sounds like a horror movie. And for caregivers, this will likely be the most hands-on part of the job.

You're helping someone get in and out of the shower, helping them wash, maybe even steadying them while they stand. If anything goes wrong, it will happen fast.

One of the biggest challenges is not just the risk of the person falling, but the caregiver falling too. If water escapes the shower and spreads across the floor, the whole bathroom suddenly becomes a hazard. If there's no seat in the shower area, you'll be bending and crouching. If there's no room to move, you'll be forced into awkward positions. Every one of those things increases the risk for everyone involved.

This again is why simple design changes can make a big difference.

Think about:

- **Wall-mounted, fold-down seat:** A shower seat will give the person being washed a break from standing and offer the caregiver more stability and control over the situation.

- **Hand-held shower:** A hand-held shower attachment will help the carer to assist with washing, make it easier for the person to wash themselves while sitting down and will simplify the cleaning of the tray or floor after showering.

- **Half-height shower screens:** Glass screens that come up to around waist height will help keep water in the shower area while allowing the caregiver to assist from outside the shower without getting soaked.

- **Low-profile or zero-threshold showers:** This keeps the shower area easy to access and safer to manage, especially if you're helping someone with mobility issues.

- **Shower controls placed within reach:** Having the controls on the opposite wall from the shower head beside the entrance means neither of you has to stretch or lean over to adjust the temperature or turn the water on or off.

A lot of the time, it's not just about the products, it's about where they are placed and how they are installed. The wrong feature in the correct position won't help anyone. The right feature, poorly installed, might actually make things worse.

Remember, it's not about adding gadgets for the sake of it. It's about making choices that have been carefully thought through and will help create a safer space for everyone involved.

A caregiver shouldn't be expected to risk an injury every time someone needs a shower. The correct setup will mean less stress and a lower chance of something going badly wrong.

Grab Bars - The Right One in the Right Place

Grab bars are one of the first things people think of when it comes to making a bathroom safer, and for good reason. But allow me to state again, "Safety in the bathroom does not come from one single item."

Just like shower trays, not all grab bars are created equal, and they're not a one-size-fits-all solution.

There's a difference between something that looks like a grab bar and something that's actually going to support the weight or pull of a grown adult. A grab bar needs to be fit for purpose and installed correctly.

The material that the grab bar is made of matters too. Some finishes are easier to grip than others. Stainless steel is a strong material, but it can be slippery and hard to grip due to the polished surface. Textured finishes, even on a round bar, make a big difference when hands are wet. Shape can also play an important part when a person's grip is weak.

I don't know about you, but as I write, I'm beginning to see a lot of similarities between shower trays and grab bars when it comes to materials and grip. Let's keep digging.

We also must consider placement. A grab bar in the wrong spot is as good as useless. It needs to be in a position that works with the way the body moves. Think about stepping into a shower, sitting down on a toilet, or pushing up from a seat. Angled bars can help with natural movement. Vertical bars might work well by the entrance. Horizontal bars can offer stability over a longer surface.

But none of this matters if the grab bar isn't installed properly. Screwed into drywall or tile with the wrong fixings? That's never going to hold up and is actually more dangerous. Every grab bar has to be installed into solid blocking or with the correct anchors. Please have them installed by someone who knows what they're doing. If a grab bar fails when someone needs it, it's too late.

There are many great options for grab bars on the market, some even have multiple functions like doubling as a towel rail. One thing's for sure, with so many choices and styles, there's no need for your bathroom to look medical because of grab bars. They're about making things safe and usable. And for caregivers, it means you're not the only thing the person has to hold on to. That in itself reduces the strain and risk for both of you.

Raised Toilets and Shower Toilets - Dignity, Hygiene, and Independence

Getting on and off the toilet is something most of us take for granted, but for anyone with reduced mobility, painful joints or perhaps balance issues, a standard height toilet can be a real problem.

Raised toilets can help solve this problem.

The higher seat makes it easier for someone to sit and stand back up, reducing the effort required. This not only helps the individual, but it also helps the caregiver at the same time. You're not having to lift or take the weight of someone quite as much, and that reduces the risk to your own back.

The big thing here can be independence. A raised toilet might just be the difference between someone needing help or managing on their own. Being able to use the toilet alone is a big deal when it comes to someone preserving their dignity.

Another great addition to the "if you can, you should" list is shower toilets. Shower toilets or seats are often overlooked, but they can be a massive help, especially for hygiene.

Shower toilets are basically a built-in washing system for your bottom, removing the need for toilet paper or wiping. This can make a huge difference for someone, for example, with arthritis or Parkinson's. Some toilets even come with heated seats and remote controls.

All in all, shower toilets make it easier for someone to stay hygienically clean without a carer needing to get involved in every detail. And that's got to be a good thing for everyone, supporting the person's dignity and independence, while reducing the physical strain and emotional awkwardness of the carer.

Lighting - Seeing the Risk Before It Happens

In bathroom safety, lighting has an important role to play but is often overlooked, especially when there's a budget to consider. But in a well-lit bathroom, you can see more clearly where you're stepping and what obstacles may be in the way. In a dimly lit bathroom, there can be a lot more guesswork. And that's when falls happen.

Good general lighting in all areas of the bathroom is important, but let's not forget task lighting. You need to be able to see clearly around the working areas, the shower, the sink, the toilet. Care needs to be taken to avoid shadowy corners or glare from shiny surfaces, which can alter depth perception, which is a problem for anyone with vision issues.

Then there's the night-time ritual that no one prepares you for. As we get older, we tend to have at least one visit to the bathroom during the night. But who wants to flick on a bright light for the 3 a.m. pee?

This is where low-level night lighting can be a great help. A soft, motion-activated light near the floor, preferably under a cabinet, can be enough to guide someone safely to and from the toilet without completely stirring them awake. It's also great for the caregiver as it will limit the number of times they might be called upon to help in the middle of the night.

Smart lighting can reduce accidents and offer better visibility for everyone.

Remember, it's about choosing the right light for the right job, in the right area.

Floor Mats - More Harm Than Help

Let's turn the conversation to floor mats, the kind you throw down outside the shower or in front of the sink. People use them to soak up water or sometimes just to warm up the cold floor where they stand. But the truth is, most of them are just an additional hazard you don't need.

It's easy to think a mat might add a level of grip, but mats can move, and the corners can curl up. This then increases the chance of a trip and a fall, which is exactly what we are trying to avoid at all costs. If the mat isn't completely fixed down or secured in place, it then becomes something you can trip over.

For caregivers, mats can be especially risky, as you're not just walking through the bathroom, you're helping someone else, you're guiding their movements and potentially carrying something like towels at the same time. You don't always have a free hand to catch yourself if something moves beneath you.

Some mats do have anti-slip backings, but these will wear down over time, and most will lose grip if water gets underneath. If you do have a floor mat in the bathroom, it must also be cleaned properly and often, as they hold moisture, which can lead to the growth of bacteria.

All mats should also be either fixed in place or designed to stay put. Better still, design the bathroom in such a way that doesn't require one. If you're caring for someone and you want to keep them on their feet and safe, look at the surface itself and avoid adding anything on top.

Vision Line Breaks - Helping the Eyes See

Vision line breaks, or color contrast in the bathroom, are something that designers should consider more often. This type of contrast is ideal for people with visual impairments or those who are experiencing a level of cognitive changes.

As we age, our depth perception can start to fade, and in a bathroom with all those same colored, shiny surfaces, it all starts to blend.

The edge of the shower, the toilet seat, the sink, they all look the same, and if everything is the same color, it's hard to judge where one thing ends and another thing starts. If the person has blurred vision and can't see clearly, that little step into the shower becomes impossible to navigate when it's a white shower tray surrounded by white floor tiles.

Adding a color contrast can help this. It doesn't have to be a bold contrast.

It can be a subtle change in tones or materials. For example:
• A slightly darker floor tile around the shower area
• A contrasting tile trim to frame out the shower tray
• Markings on glass screens so people don't walk into them
• A colored grab bar instead of a white one that disappears against the white tiles

Subtle changes can make navigation a lot easier for both the person being cared for and the caregiver who's helping them. Design with purpose!

Shower Seating

Standing in the shower takes energy. It's tiring.

The warm water will begin to raise the body's core temperature, and the body will then start working overtime to cool itself down. Simultaneously, it will trigger signals from the brain that make us sleepy and fatigued.

For someone with reduced mobility or poor balance, this can feel like too much and cause weakness. For a caregiver trying to wash or support that person, it becomes a balancing act.

This is where a fit-for-purpose shower seat becomes a real game-changer.

Any shower seat should be foldable, fixed to the wall and extremely secure. It has to offer the user the confidence to sit down without worrying that it will come away from the wall. When the seat is not in use, it should also have the capability to be folded away so it doesn't cause interference for other users.

Look for a seat that is strong and easy to clean.

Portable shower chairs are an option, especially if the bathroom is shared or the seat needs to be moved around. It should have rubber feet and fit properly inside the shower space.

From a caregiver's perspective, having the person seated:
• Makes it easier to assist with washing
• Reduces the risk of the person falling
• Removes the stress of keeping the person upright

It's probably one of the most practical safety upgrades you can add to a shower, and once again, it's not about making the bathroom look hospital-like or clinical. Manufacturers are very aware of this, and there are some really nice seats with high-level design on the market.

Fit for Purpose - And Installed Correctly

Some products on a shelf or in a brochure can look amazing, but when they're installed in the real world, they're just not up to the job. That's why I will tell you over and over again:

Whatever you choose for a bathroom must be fit for purpose, and it must be installed correctly. There's no room for "good enough" when it comes to safety. If something is designed to support a person's weight, it has to be anchored into the wall properly. If something is going to be walked on with bare feet when it's wet and soapy, it has to have the highest levels of anti-slip properties available. If something is going to be used every day, it has to be easily cleaned.

Installation standards are critical. A great product, badly fitted, is a liability. A grab bar that pulls off the wall. A shower tray that isn't sealed properly. A toilet seat that shifts under pressure. All of these create danger, not safety. Always hire a professional who knows what they are doing.

Spend money where it counts. If the budget is limited, then prioritize. Do fewer things but do them right. Safety, reliability and peace of mind for both the person using the bathroom and the person helping them - that's what it's all about.

Bathroom Safety Checklist for Caregivers

If you're not entirely sure where to start, here's a practical checklist to help you think through what's needed.

Surfaces
• Is the shower or bathroom floor genuinely anti-slip?
• Can the surfaces be cleaned easily?
• Are you aware of what products can and can't be used on it?
• Is there visible soap or shampoo build-up creating additional risk?

Shower
• Is there a seat (preferably wall-mounted) to reduce standing time?
• Are the shower controls within reach from outside and inside?
• Does water stay inside the shower area, or is it pooling where it shouldn't?

Grab Bars
• Are grab bars placed where they're needed most?
• Can they support full body weight?
• Were they professionally installed into blocking or with proper anchors?

Toilet
• Is the toilet seat at a comfortable height?
• Would a raised toilet or wash-and-dry seat help support independence?
• Is the user struggling to stand or clean themselves properly?

Lighting
• Is there enough general lighting in the room?
• Are there night lights or soft motion-sensor lighting for overnight use?
• Are shadows or glare creating visual confusion?

Visibility
• Are key features easily identifiable through color contrast?
• Are there markings on glass screens to show where they start and stop?
• Can someone with low vision navigate the space with minimal guidance?

Other Hazards
• Are mats removed or secured safely to the floor?
• Is the floor clear of clutter?
• Has everything been tested from a seated and standing position?

If any of these questions raise a red flag, that's the place to begin. Every small improvement will add up.

Final Words - From One Professional to Another

I've spent a lifetime working on or in bathrooms. I've seen bad ones, good ones and everything in between. However, the one constant I keep coming back to is that a safe bathroom benefits everybody. The person being cared for and the person doing the caring.

If you're a caregiver by choice, by profession, or by circumstance, you already have enough going on, and you shouldn't also have to be worrying about slippery floors or poor lighting. You shouldn't be lifting someone out of the shower and hoping your foot doesn't slip.

That's not safe and it's not right.

If you take nothing else from this chapter, make it this:
• Be confident to take action
• Push for the changes that will have the biggest impact
• Don't cut corners
• You don't need to do everything at once
• Use a professional for installation

One slip or fall can change someone's life - preventing that fall can also change their life.

[7]

Aging in Place Starts in the Medicine Cabinet

By
Dr. DeLon Canterbury

The phrase "aging in place" often brings to mind images of well-lit hallways, sturdy grab bars, and cozy living rooms where older adults can enjoy familiar surroundings for decades. But there's another side to independence that rarely makes the glossy brochures, a side hidden in plain sight, tucked into the kitchen drawer or bathroom shelf: the medications.

For Dr. DeLon Canterbury, this unseen world became the heart of his life's work. As a pharmacist, he knew the statistics. As a clinician, he'd seen the consequences. And as a human being, he understood the deep desire for older adults to *live well*, not just longer, in the homes they love.

One afternoon, in a small community clinic with the fluorescent hum that healthcare workers know all too well, he met a woman in her eighties holding a paper bag of prescription bottles. Some were unopened. Some were duplicates. A few were for conditions she no longer had. On paper, she was "managed" by her care team. In reality, she was dizzy, confused, and fearful of another trip to the emergency room.

This wasn't a rare occurrence. For Dr. Canterbury, it was Tuesday.

The encounter was a turning point, not because it was his first case of overprescribing, but because it laid bare the human cost. Her son had missed work repeatedly to take her to appointments. Her granddaughter was learning about the healthcare system through trial and error. The patient herself had lost confidence in her own body.

"Aging in place," Dr. Canterbury thought, "isn't possible when someone's trapped in a cycle of medication side effects, ER visits, and fear."

From a Note in the Margin to a Mission

The seed for GeriatRx wasn't born in a corporate boardroom, it started as a scribble in the margins of a notepad between "call back insurance rep" and "fix printer."

The idea was deceptively simple:

• Review each medication a patient takes.
• Remove those that are no longer needed, effective, or safe.
• Do it in a way that centers the patient's life, not just their lab results.

In the healthcare world, however, simple ideas often run head-first into complex systems. Dr. Canterbury knew that if deprescribing was going to stick, it needed to be more than a clinical service, it needed to be a movement.

So, he built GeriatRx with four guiding values:

• **Compassion:** Meet patients where they are, whether that's in their living room or on a video call.
• **Honesty:** Have real conversations about what's working and what's not.
• **Education:** Empower patients and caregivers by explaining the "why" behind every change.
• **Transparency:** Keep costs, processes, and outcomes clear and understandable.

These principles aligned naturally with the pillars of the National Aging in Place Council (NAIPC) particularly health and wellness, finances, and social connection. After all, when unnecessary medications are removed, people not only feel better, but they can also move more freely, engage more fully, and manage expenses more effectively.

Polypharmacy: The Quiet Barrier to Independence

Polypharmacy, the use of multiple medications, isn't just a line in a medical chart. For older adults, it can be the silent saboteur of independence.

Research shows that nearly 40% of adults over 65 take five or more medications. With each additional prescription, the risk of drug interactions, cognitive impairment, and falls rises. Falls, in turn, are a leading cause of hospitalization and loss of independence in this population.

In other words: if the goal is to keep people safe and well at home, medication safety has to be part of the plan. Yet, in many care settings, no single provider takes responsibility for reviewing the entire medication list in the context of a patient's overall life.

GeriatRx steps into that gap, not to eliminate medication use entirely, but to make sure every pill taken is still the right one, at the right dose, for the right reason.

The Dr. Canterbury Approach

What sets Dr. Canterbury apart isn't just his clinical skill, it's his ability to navigate the human side of healthcare.

He can translate complex pharmacology into everyday language without making patients or families feel overwhelmed. He can speak in the boardroom about cost savings and in the church hall about protecting "grandma's clarity." He listens as much as he advises.

Importantly, he doesn't see deprescribing as an isolated act, it's part of a larger web of care that includes physicians, nurses, caregivers, and community resources. By building trust with all of them, he ensures changes aren't just made, but sustained.

While GeriatRx specializes in medication management, its impact touches the NAIPC Pillars:

• **Health & Wellness:** Reducing unnecessary medications can improve mobility, cognition, and overall vitality.
• **Finances:** Fewer prescriptions mean lower costs, both for patients and the healthcare system.
• **Housing:** Preventing falls and confusion supports safer living environments.
• **Social Interaction:** Clearer thinking and better physical stability encourage participation in community life.

This is the subtle but powerful role deprescribing plays in aging in place, it's the behind-the-scenes work that makes the visible aspects of independence possible.

A typical day might include reviewing a patient's medication list, collaborating with their physician to taper a high-risk drug, and educating the family on what to expect. It might also involve advocating with an insurance company for coverage of a safer alternative or training other clinicians on deprescribing best practices.

And sometimes, it's about celebrating small wins: a patient calling to say she can garden again without dizziness, or a caregiver sharing that mom's mood has lifted since a sedating medication was reduced.

Humor has its place, too. Dr. Canterbury jokes that while there's no reality show called *America's Next Top Pill Cutter*, there should be, because the transformations are real.

Why This Work Matters Now

The aging population in the U.S. is growing rapidly. By 2030, one in five Americans will be 65 or older. More people will want, and need, to age in place. The challenge is that the healthcare system hasn't fully adapted to support this shift, especially when it comes to medication safety.

Deprescribing is one of the most cost-effective, immediately impactful interventions we have to help older adults stay safe at home. It reduces hospitalizations, improves daily functioning, and strengthens the very foundation NAIPC is built on: proactive planning for a better quality of life.

Dr. Canterbury knows this isn't quick work. Changing how medications are managed requires persistence, education, and collaboration at every level, from individual providers to policy makers.

But every success story builds momentum. Every patient who regains balance or mental clarity is proof that this approach works. And every partnership with community organizations, healthcare systems, or NAIPC chapters brings the vision of safer, healthier aging in place closer to reality.

If aging in place is a house, medication safety is the foundation. You can have the best design, the sturdiest walls, and the most beautiful view, but if the foundation is unstable, the rest won't hold.

Through GeriatRx, Dr. DeLon Canterbury is quietly, persistently reinforcing that foundation, one patient, one family, one conversation at a time. And in doing so, he's helping make the NAIPC vision not just an aspiration, but an attainable reality for the people who need it most.

Building the Movement

The early days of GeriatRx didn't have a grand office, a massive team, or a big marketing budget. What it did have was momentum, and that momentum was fueled by one thing, *results*. Every time a patient experienced fewer side effects, regained the ability to walk without fear of falling, or simply felt more like themselves again, word began to spread. Slowly at first, but steadily enough that the phone started ringing more often.

Dr. DeLon Canterbury's work was never meant to exist in isolation. From the start, he knew that deprescribing needed to be part of a broader movement, one that reached into communities, care facilities, and the healthcare system itself. You can't shift a culture by changing one patient's regimen at a time. You have to build an environment where questioning the necessity of medications becomes as routine as checking blood pressure.

Partnerships began forming naturally. Home care agencies recognized that reducing unnecessary medications not only improved patient safety but made their work easier and more rewarding. Hospitals saw potential in cutting readmissions. Families who had struggled to manage complex medication schedules found relief in knowing someone was finally looking at the whole picture. Each new collaboration added another link to a growing chain of advocates.

Of course, this kind of work is never without its challenges. In a healthcare system designed to treat problems as they arise, the idea of stepping back and removing treatments can be a hard sell. There's an ingrained belief, both among patients and providers, that more medicine means better care. Convincing people otherwise requires patience, data, and no small amount of diplomacy. There are also the bureaucratic hurdles, insurance coverage, prescribing rules, and policies that aren't designed with deprescribing in mind. Sometimes the work feels like trying to untangle a knot that's been tied for decades.

But knots can be untied. And often, the way forward isn't to pull harder but to find the right angle. Dr. Canterbury has become skilled at this, presenting the benefits in ways that resonate with whoever is in the room. For a physician, that might mean citing research on reduced hospitalization rates. For a caregiver, it's the promise of fewer stressful nights managing side effects. For patients, it's about regaining independence, energy, and clarity.

Inside GeriatRx, the day-to-day is a blend of science and storytelling. Reviewing a medication list isn't just an exercise in clinical judgment, it's also about listening to the person behind that list. There's the patient who thought her constant fatigue was "just getting older" until a medication change lifted the fog. The man who gave up driving because of dizziness, only to get back behind the wheel after a safe dose reduction. The grandmother who can now keep up with her grandchildren without feeling winded halfway through a walk.

These are not just medical adjustments; they're life changes. And they ripple outward. A patient who can move more freely might join a community group again, reducing isolation. A caregiver with fewer daily medication tasks has more time to simply be present with their loved one. Independence is not just preserved, it's restored.

Education is a key part of the movement. GeriatRx doesn't just make changes; it explains them, teaching patients and families how to ask the right questions and spot potential issues early. Workshops for community groups, training for healthcare staff, and the Deprescribing Accelerator program for clinicians all serve the same purpose, spreading the knowledge so that deprescribing becomes part of the culture, not just a specialized service.

Technology has played its part too. Using platforms like Practice Better, GeriatRx can connect with patients virtually, making care accessible for those who may be homebound or live in rural areas. Secure messaging, virtual consultations, and shared care plans mean that medication management isn't limited by geography. It also means caregivers can be looped in more easily, ensuring continuity and trust.

But for all the tools and strategies, there's still a deeply human core to this work. One of the most telling moments came when a patient's daughter told Dr. Canterbury, "You gave me my mom back." She wasn't talking about curing a disease. She was talking about clearing the mental fog, the physical unsteadiness, and the constant worry that had crept in over years of unnecessary medication. That's the kind of feedback that makes the late nights, the policy headaches, and the uphill battles worth it.

Changing the Script on Aging in Place

When you step back and look at the whole picture, one truth becomes clear: aging in place isn't just about where we live. It's about how we live.

Yes, the conversation often starts with housing, whether a home is accessible, safe, and well-maintained. But if the body and mind aren't functioning at their best, even the safest house can feel like a prison. This is where the work of Dr. DeLon Canterbury and GeriatRx finds its purpose: protecting the independence and quality of life that aging in place promises, by tackling one of its most overlooked barriers, unnecessary or harmful medication use.

The journey here has been both straightforward and winding. Straightforward in its logic, fewer unnecessary medications mean fewer side effects, fewer falls, fewer hospitalizations, and more vitality. Winding in its execution, because changing healthcare habits is like steering a massive ship with a pocket-sized rudder. It takes persistence, patience, and proof.

It began with a spark: a patient weighed down by a bag of prescriptions, a family unsure what was necessary and what was harming more than helping. That moment led to a mission, one that grew through partnerships, patient victories, and community education. Over time, it has expanded into a vision for the future: a healthcare culture where deprescribing is standard practice, technology supports safer medication use, and communities are equipped to advocate for themselves.

The connection to aging in place is undeniable. Deprescribing lives at the intersection of health, safety, and independence. It's preventive care in the truest sense, protecting older adults before a preventable crisis sends them to the emergency room or forces them to leave their home. It's financial stewardship, reducing prescription costs and avoiding expensive hospitalizations. It's social connection, because a clearer mind and steadier body open the door to engagement, relationships, and joy.

One of the most striking things about this work is how personal it is. Yes, there's science. Yes, there's data. But at its heart, deprescribing is about individual lives and the ripple effect each improvement has. A patient regains their balance and can now walk to the neighbor's house for coffee. That daily interaction lifts mood, eases loneliness, and even boosts physical health. A caregiver spends less time managing a confusing medication regimen and more time simply enjoying their loved one's company. These are the moments that make independence meaningful.

It's easy to underestimate the emotional toll polypharmacy takes, not just on patients, but on entire families. Caregivers carry the weight of uncertainty: Is Mom's forgetfulness from age, or from that new pill? Did Dad fall because of a hazard in the house, or because his blood pressure medication was too strong? When medication safety becomes part of the aging-in-place conversation, those questions get clearer answers. And when the answers are clear, the solutions are better.

The challenge now is scale. One pharmacist, no matter how driven, cannot change an entire system alone. But one pharmacist can prove it's possible, and then create the blueprint for others to follow. GeriatRx is already moving in that direction, with clinician training, technology integration, and partnerships across sectors. The goal is not to own the movement, but to accelerate it.

Scaling also means reshaping the public narrative. Right now, the prevailing assumption is that aging will naturally come with a growing list of prescriptions. Shifting that mindset will take time, just as it took time for the public to accept that seat belts save lives or that smoking is dangerous. It will require public education, advocacy, and consistent reinforcement from healthcare providers.

That's where NAIPC and its network can make a profound difference. With chapters across the country, a trusted reputation, and deep community ties, NAIPC is uniquely positioned to bring deprescribing into everyday aging-in-place conversations. It doesn't have to be a standalone topic, it can be woven into wellness workshops, home safety assessments, and financial planning discussions. The message is simple: safe, appropriate medication use is part of aging well at home.

The road ahead will require practical steps. On the clinical side, deprescribing needs to be baked into care protocols. On the policy side, it needs recognition and reimbursement from insurers. On the community side, it needs champions, professionals, family members, and older adults themselves, who are willing to ask the hard questions and push for safer, simpler care.

There's reason to be optimistic. More healthcare providers are learning about deprescribing. Patients are coming to appointments armed with questions. Families are speaking up about side effects and quality of life. And most importantly, those changes are translating into measurable results: fewer hospitalizations, better mobility, improved mental clarity, and a stronger sense of independence.

What GeriatRx represents is a shift in focus, from adding more to doing better. From treating aging as an inevitable decline to treating it as a stage of life that can be vibrant, engaged, and fulfilling. From assuming that "more medication equals better care" to recognizing that sometimes, the best prescription is one less.

As this chapter closes, it's worth returning to that early image: the older woman with the bag of medications, unsure which ones she really needed. She could be anyone's mother, aunt, or neighbor. And somewhere in every community, there's another person just like her. The difference now is that we have a clearer path forward. We have the tools, the knowledge, and the growing will to act.

The baton is in our hands. The question is what we'll do with it. Will we keep the conversation going? Will we make medication safety a standard part of aging-in-place planning? Will we use our roles, whether as healthcare providers, community leaders, family members, or advocates, to push this vision forward?

The answer should be yes. Because when we choose to act, we're not just reducing pill counts, we're giving people back their mornings, their walks, their laughter, and their confidence. We're protecting the independence they've worked for their whole lives. And we're making sure that aging in place is not just a place, but a life worth living.

That is the change worth making. That is the horizon worth chasing. And that is the legacy we can build together.

What Caregivers Can Do Today

Deprescribing might sound like something only a pharmacist or doctor can tackle, but caregivers are often the spark that gets the process started. Medication safety at home doesn't require a medical degree, just curiosity, attentiveness, and persistence. Whether you're caring for a parent, spouse, or neighbor, there are simple but powerful actions you can take to help protect their health.

Five Best Practice for Addressing Medication Concerns:

1. **Keep a Current Medication List:** Write down every prescription, over-the-counter medicine, vitamin, and supplement. Update it after each doctor's visit or pharmacy refill.

2. **Ask the Right Questions:** For each medication, ask: *Why is this needed? What's the lowest effective dose? Are there safer alternatives? What happens if we reduce or stop it?*

3. **Know the Red Flags:** Learn about tools like the Beers Criteria developed by the *American Geriatrics Society*, which lists medicines that may cause more harm than good in older adults. Even without memorizing it, awareness of its existence can spark valuable conversations.

4. **Watch for Changes:** Track new symptoms, side effects, or shifts in mood, balance, or memory. Even small changes can point to a medication issue.

5. **Stay Connected:** Coordinate with all healthcare providers to ensure the care plan is aligned. Some clinicians use the ViONE model, a structured framework for identifying and prioritizing deprescribing opportunities, to guide decisions and make medication reviews more efficient.

These small, everyday actions, paired with a growing national awareness, build momentum — and momentum has a way of attracting more momentum.

Still, building a movement requires more than passion and good intentions. It requires infrastructure. That means establishing workflows that can scale, training additional pharmacists and clinicians, and developing clear models that can be adopted in other settings. It also means finding sustainable funding, whether through insurance reimbursement, grants, or partnerships, that ensures the work doesn't depend solely on one person's energy.

The cultural shift is gradual, but it's happening. More healthcare professionals are beginning to see deprescribing as a proactive, preventive measure rather than an afterthought. Families are more willing to speak up about concerns. Patients are starting to ask, "Do I still need this?" And when that question becomes commonplace, the movement will have truly taken hold.

For now, the work continues one conversation at a time. Sometimes those conversations happen in a patient's home, surrounded by family photos and the scent of fresh coffee. Sometimes they happen in a hospital conference room, with charts and data projected on a screen. And sometimes they happen in places you wouldn't expect, at community events, church gatherings, or even while standing in line at the grocery store when someone recognizes Dr. Canterbury and wants to talk about their medication list.

This is how change spreads, not through a single sweeping reform, but through hundreds of small, meaningful interactions that shift the way people think about health and independence. GeriatRx is part of that shift, and every patient story adds to the growing proof that this work matters.

Making aging in place safe and fulfilling depends on restoring confidence—in patients, in families, and in the healthcare system's ability to serve them well. The progress is real. What began as one pharmacist's determination to fix a recurring problem is now part of a larger, nationwide effort to redefine what good care looks like for older adults. With persistence, collaboration, and a focus on what truly matters, even the most entrenched habits in healthcare can be transformed.

The Horizon Ahead

The work of deprescribing is not just about taking away pills; it's about giving back possibilities.

When you've spent years staring down the tangle of modern medication use in older adults, you learn to celebrate small wins. The patient who's finally able to walk their dog again without feeling lightheaded. The daughter who no longer spends her Sundays sorting 14 different pill bottles. The son who tells you his mother's laughter has returned.

But there comes a point when you realize that small wins, while precious, aren't enough. If we want systemic change, real, lasting, wide-scale change, those wins have to be multiplied, scaled, and embedded into the way healthcare operates.

That's the horizon Dr. DeLon Canterbury sees. It's not a vague dream; it's a clear map. The goal is nothing less than making deprescribing a standard of care, not an optional add-on. It's about creating a healthcare culture where the question "Do you still need this medication?" is asked as often as "What's your blood pressure?"

The vision is bold. GeriatRx is poised to expand its reach beyond individual consultations and local partnerships, developing models that can be adopted by healthcare systems, senior living communities, and public health agencies across the country. That means refining protocols, creating easy-to-use training modules for clinicians, and building digital tools.

Technology will play a bigger role in what's coming. Imagine a platform that integrates with electronic health records and sends alerts when a patient's medication list grows past a certain threshold. Imagine caregivers receiving plain-language explanations about why a certain medication might be risky and what safer options exist. Imagine a national deprescribing database that tracks outcomes and helps identify patterns across different populations. These tools aren't pipe dreams, they're already on the whiteboard, being sketched, tested, and prepared for rollout.

But tech alone won't make the shift. The heart of this work is still human. The future of GeriatRx involves training a new wave of healthcare professionals who see deprescribing not as a fringe skill but as a core competency. Through programs like the Deprescribing Accelerator, pharmacists, nurses, and physicians will learn not only the clinical steps but also the communication skills needed to have these conversations with empathy and clarity.

Community engagement will deepen too. Partnering with NAIPC chapters, senior centers, and local organizations can bring deprescribing education directly into the neighborhoods where it's needed most. Workshops, webinars, and resource kits can equip older adults and their families to advocate for themselves in medical settings. This isn't just outreach, it's empowerment. Because when patients and caregivers understand their options, they're more likely to speak up and less likely to accept "just take this" without question.

There's also a policy dimension on the horizon. For deprescribing to become mainstream, it needs to be recognized, and reimbursed, by insurers and government programs. That means building a compelling case with data: showing how reducing unnecessary medications cuts hospitalizations, lowers costs, and improves quality of life. The evidence exists; now it needs to be presented in ways that influence decision-makers. Dr. Canterbury has already been part of conversations at the state and national level, and the plan is to keep that momentum going.

On the nonprofit side, there's enormous potential for grant-funded initiatives that bring deprescribing services to underserved communities. Many of the patients who most need this work are the least able to access it. By partnering with foundations, public health departments, and philanthropic organizations, GeriatRx can close that gap, ensuring that safe medication use isn't a privilege but a standard.

And then there's the bigger cultural shift, the one that moves beyond healthcare policy and into everyday life. Right now, the default assumption is that aging comes with an ever-growing list of prescriptions. Changing that assumption will take time, but it's possible. We've seen it happen before with smoking, with seat belts, with routine exercise. The more people see deprescribing as a normal, responsible step in aging well, the more momentum the movement will have.

This next chapter for GeriatRx will require more voices, more allies, and more courage. It will require healthcare professionals who are willing to rethink old habits, caregivers who are ready to ask hard questions, and community leaders who will champion the cause. It will also require resilience, because shifting any entrenched system comes with resistance.

But here's the thing, resistance is often a sign that you're doing something that matters. And if there's one thing the journey so far has proven, it's that this matters. Every patient story is proof. Every fall prevented, every moment of clarity regained, every dollar saved from unnecessary prescriptions is a reminder that the work is worth it.

Dr. Canterbury often says that deprescribing is about "giving people back their time." Not just in the sense of years added to life, but in the day-to-day moments, the walks, the conversations, the hobbies, the laughter, that make life rich and meaningful. That's the real horizon. It's not just a future with fewer pills; it's a future with more life in it.

In the coming years, the goal is for GeriatRx to be more than a practice. It will be a blueprint. Other pharmacists and healthcare teams will be able to adopt its methods, tailor them to their communities, and keep the movement growing. The hope is that one day, the term "deprescribing" won't need explaining, it will be as familiar and uncontroversial as "check your blood pressure."

Standing at this point in the journey, it's hard not to feel excited. The past has shown what's possible on a small scale. The present is proving that the demand and the need are there. And the future? The future is about scale, systems, and making sure that safe, thoughtful medication management becomes an unquestioned part of aging in place.

It's not just about medicine. It's about dignity, independence, and the simple human right to live the later chapters of life with clarity and strength. And that's a horizon worth running toward because the future of aging in place should be one where health, independence, and dignity are the norm, not the exception.

[8]
Aging in Motion: Staying Active with Mobility Supports

By
Cindi Petito

Introduction

As we journey through life, the concept of aging transforms into a vibrant celebration of experiences, wisdom, and growth. "Aging in Motion: Staying Active with Mobility Supports?" invites us to explore the dynamic and enriching aspects of senior living, particularly through the lens of mobility. As we age, maintaining mobility becomes essential for independence and quality of life, and this is where mobility aids and devices play a crucial role.

From canes and walkers to scooters and wheelchairs, these tools empower older adults to navigate their homes and communities safely and confidently, fostering social connections and encouraging an active lifestyle. However, it is not just about acquiring this equipment; it is equally important to ensure that mobility devices are conducive to use in home and community environments.

In home settings, the design and size of mobility aids must align with the layout of living spaces, allowing for easy maneuverability through doorways, hallways, and rooms. Features such as lightweight materials and compact designs enhance usability and comfort, ensuring we can move freely and safely within our homes.

In community settings, accessibility becomes paramount. Sidewalks, public transportation, and recreational facilities must accommodate the diverse needs of older adults using mobility devices. This includes considerations for curb cuts, ramps, and spacious pathways that facilitate seamless navigation. Prioritizing accessible environments empowers individuals to engage fully in their communities, participate in social activities, and maintain meaningful connections with family and friends.

By embracing mobility aids and devices and ensuring they are suitable for home and community use, we enhance our physical capabilities and unlock the potential for adventure and fulfillment throughout later life.

What Are Mobility Aids?

Mobility aids are essential devices that support older adults in maintaining their independence, safety, and quality of life as physical abilities naturally change over time. As people age, they may experience a gradual decline in strength, balance, coordination, and endurance, which may create new challenges in walking and mobility. Mobility aids are designed to support physical changes and maintain independence, helping older adults stay active, reduce the risk of falls, and continue participating in daily activities both at home and in the community. In essence, mobility aids are not just devices, they are gateways to freedom and dignity in the aging process.

As individuals experience challenges in ambulation or walking, mobility aids and devices become essential devices for quality of life. These devices are not just about movement, they are about empowerment. They allow individuals to remain active, engage socially, and retain autonomy, even as physical abilities change. By introducing the right mobility aid at the right time, we can support safe walking behaviors.

Here's how they relate to these changes:

Understanding Ambulation and Potential Changes with Age
• Ambulation refers to the ability to walk independently.
• With age or certain health conditions (e.g., arthritis, Parkinson's, stroke recovery), people may experience:
  - Slower walking
  - Fatigue or reduced endurance
  - Changes in coordination
  - Decreased muscle strength
  - Increased risk of falls

These changes often occur gradually, making early intervention with appropriate mobility support crucial.

Walking aids range from simple equipment like canes or walking sticks to more advanced devices such as walkers, rollators (walker with a seat), wheelchairs, motorized scooters. Each type serves a specific purpose, whether it's providing balance, reducing strain on joints, or enabling full mobility for those with significantly limited physical function. Mobility devices are not one-size-fits-all; they are tailored to meet the unique needs of individuals based on their physical condition, environment, and lifestyle. By supporting movement both at home and in the community, these devices play a vital role in enhancing quality of life, promoting social engagement, and empowering individuals to age with confidence and dignity.

Types of Mobility Aids and Their Uses

Mobility aids, also called Mobility Assistive Equipment (MAE), refer to a broad category of devices designed to help individuals with physical limitations move more freely, safely, and independently.

Canes and Crutches

Canes come in several types, each designed to meet different mobility needs. Standard (straight) canes offer basic support and are ideal for individuals with mild balance issues. Quad canes have a four-point base for added stability, making them suitable for users who need more support. Folding canes are lightweight and portable, perfect for occasional use or travel. Each type helps improve mobility and safety, depending on the user's physical condition and environment.

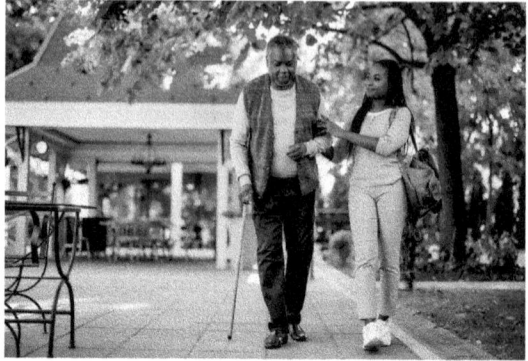

Forearm crutches are a valuable mobility aid, especially those with limited hand strength who may struggle with traditional canes or underarm crutches. Unlike canes and standard crutches that rely heavily on hand grip and wrist strength, forearm crutches distribute weight more evenly across the forearm and upper arm, reducing strain on the hands and wrists. This makes them particularly suitable for individuals with arthritis, neurological conditions, or recovering from injuries that affect grip strength.

Walkers

Walkers are essential mobility aids that offer varying levels of support depending on their design. Standard walkers typically have four legs with rubber tips and no wheels, providing maximum stability and support. However, some standard walkers come with two wheels in the front, allowing smoother movement while still offering substantial

stability, which is ideal for users who need support but find lifting the walker difficult. Three-wheeled walkers feature a triangular frame with one wheel in front and two in the back. They may be more maneuverable than four-wheeled models but offer less stability for individuals with balance impairments. Choosing the right walker depends on the user's physical needs, environment, and comfort with balance.

Four Wheeled Walkers (Walkers with a Seat)

Four-wheeled walkers with a seat, also known as rollators or carriage walkers, are advanced mobility aids designed for individuals who need support and a place to rest. They feature four wheels for smooth movement, hand brakes for safety, and a built-in seat that allows users to take breaks when needed. Many models also include a storage pouch or basket for carrying personal items. Rollators are ideal for active people with mild to moderate mobility challenges who spend time indoors and outdoors. While they offer less stability than standard walkers, their convenience and versatility make them popular for maintaining independence. Because these walkers have four wheels and roll easily, they may move ahead of the user unintentionally, increasing the chance of instability or falls if not adequately controlled. Proper training and assessment are essential to ensure safe use.

Manual Wheelchairs

Manual wheelchairs are mobility devices that require the user to propel themselves using their arms and/or feet, or be pushed by a caregiver. They are not powered by motors and rely entirely on physical effort for movement. These wheelchairs typically feature large rear wheels with hand rims for self-propulsion and smaller front wheels for steering. Manual wheelchairs are available in various styles, including lightweight and foldable models for easy transport and more durable designs for long-term use. They offer independence for users with sufficient upper body strength and coordination. They offer independence for users with sufficient upper body strength and coordination.

One common type is the transport chair, which is lighter and more compact than standard manual wheelchairs. Transport chairs have four small rear wheels and are designed specifically to be pushed by a caregiver, making them ideal for short trips, medical appointments, or situations where the user cannot self-propel.

Motorized Scooters

Motorized scooters are powered mobility devices designed for individuals who have difficulty walking long distances but can still sit upright and operate controls with their arms and hands. They come in three-wheel and four-wheel models. Three-wheel scooters offer greater maneuverability and a tighter turning radius. On the other hand, four-wheel scooters provide enhanced stability and are better suited for outdoor terrain or uneven surfaces. Both types feature a seat, tiller with steering controls, and rechargeable batteries.

Many scooters are designed with portability in mind. Portable scooter models can be disassembled into multiple parts for easy transport in a car or storage. In contrast, others are larger and cannot

be disassembled, requiring a vehicle lift system to transport them in the community. Choosing the right scooter depends on the user's mobility needs, lifestyle, and transportation options.

While portable motorized scooters offer convenience for users, they can present significant challenges for caregivers, especially when frequent disassembly and reassembly are required throughout the day. These scooters often break down into multiple parts, such as the seat, battery, and base, which must be lifted and placed into a vehicle. This task demands physical strength, coordination, and time, which can be taxing if repeated multiple times during a single outing. Additionally, inclement weather like rain, snow, or extreme heat can make the process uncomfortable or unsafe, especially when loading or unloading in outdoor parking areas. For caregivers, choosing a scooter should involve evaluating the user's needs and the practicality and physical demands of transport and setup.

Although portable scooter parts are designed to be manageable, their individual weights can still be substantial, especially for caregivers who must lift and load them repeatedly.

Here's a general breakdown of approximate weight ranges for each part:
• Seat: 15–25 lbs
• Battery pack: 20–35 lbs (some models have dual batteries)
• Base/frame: 35–50 lbs (often the heaviest part)
• Tiller/steering column: 10–20 lbs

Even though these weights are distributed to make transport easier, lifting them into a car trunk or SUV can be physically demanding—especially for caregivers with limited strength or mobility.

While motorized scooters are sufficient for outdoor travel and spacious indoor environments, they can be challenging to maneuver in tight indoor spaces such as small apartments, narrow hallways, or crowded public areas.

Their larger turning radius and longer frame make navigating corners and doorways challenging. In contrast, power wheelchairs discussed in the next section are specifically designed for tight indoor mobility, offering a compact frame and precise control through a joystick or other adaptive input. They typically have a much smaller turning radius, allowing users to move easily in confined areas. If a person's primary mobility needs are indoors, especially in small or cluttered living spaces, a power wheelchair is often the better choice for safety, comfort, and independence.

Power Wheelchairs

Power wheelchairs are motorized mobility devices designed for individuals who cannot propel a manual wheelchair or safely operate a motorized scooter due to limited strength, coordination, or endurance. These wheelchairs are powered by rechargeable batteries and controlled using a joystick or alternative driving methods, such as sip-and-puff systems or

head controls, depending on the user's abilities. Power wheelchairs offer enhanced independence and can be customized with features like reclining seats, elevating leg rests, and advanced suspension for comfort and terrain adaptability. While they provide significant mobility benefits, they are typically heavier and less portable than manual wheelchairs, requiring accessible transportation options and proper storage space. Power wheelchairs are ideal for full-time users who need reliable, long-distance mobility both indoors and outdoors.

Seating is a critical factor in choosing a power wheelchair, both for comfort and medical support. Two options are captain's seats and custom seating systems, each serving different needs. Captain's seats are standard, padded seats that resemble car seats. They typically include adjustable armrests, a reclining back, and a swivel base for easier transfers. These seats suit individuals who need basic comfort and support for shorter durations or occasional use. They are often found on consumer-grade power wheelchairs and are ideal for those with mild to moderate mobility needs.

In contrast, custom seating systems are designed for individuals with complex medical conditions, postural challenges, or those who spend extended periods in wheelchairs. These systems are built to fit the body precisely and may include features like contoured cushions, lateral supports, headrests, and pressure-relieving materials. They help prevent pressure sores, improve posture, and enhance overall function and comfort. Choosing between the two depends on the mobility level, medical needs, and daily usage.

It is highly recommended that older adults undergo a professional evaluation by a mobility specialist, such as an occupational therapist, physical therapist, or a certified assistive technology professional (ATP), before selecting a mobility device. These specialists assess the individual's daily functional needs, physical abilities, home environment, and lifestyle to determine which device will provide the best support, safety, and independence. Whether it's a cane, walker, scooter, or power wheelchair, the right choice depends on factors like balance, endurance, strength, and cognitive function. A personalized evaluation helps avoid inappropriate equipment that could lead to discomfort, injury, or reduced mobility, and ensures the device truly enhances the person's quality of life.

When To Consider a Mobility Aid?

We should consider using a mobility aid when experiencing challenges that affect our safety, independence, or ability to perform daily activities comfortably. Warning signs include frequent falls, a growing fear of falling, difficulty walking for extended periods, or relying on furniture and walls for support. Health conditions such as recovering from surgery, arthritis, loss of endurance, progressive joint and muscle pain, or neurological disorders like Parkinson's disease can impair balance and strength, making mobility aids especially beneficial. Additionally, if we start avoiding social outings or daily tasks due to mobility concerns, tools like canes, walkers, or scooters can help restore confidence and independence. While some may feel hesitant, viewing mobility aids as a loss of autonomy, these devices are tools that enhance freedom by enabling safer and more active lifestyles.

Mobility assistive equipment (MAE) plays a critical role in helping older adults avoid falls, which are a leading cause of injury and loss of independence in older adults. Mobility aids, provide physical support by redistributing body weight, offering a wider base of stability, and reducing pressure on painful joints. They also serve as psychological support, boosting confidence and reducing anxiety about walking or standing. For example, canes are suitable for individuals with mild balance issues, while quad canes and offset canes offer enhanced stability. Walkers, especially those with wheels, are ideal for those needing full weight-bearing support and help prevent falls during movement or transitions between surfaces. Using the right aid can significantly reduce the likelihood of falls by improving posture, gait, and overall mobility.

The Fall Prevention Foundation emphasizes the critical role mobility aids play in reducing fall risks among older adults. The Foundation's comprehensive guide highlights how walking aids offer both physical and psychological support. Physically, these devices help redistribute body weight, provide a wider base of support, and reduce pressure on painful joints. Psychologically, they instill confidence and reduce anxiety about movement, which can otherwise lead to inactivity and isolation. The Foundation also addresses the stigma some older adults feel about using mobility aids, encouraging a shift in perspective: these tools are not signs of weakness but empowering devices that promote independence and safety (Fall Prevention Foundation, 2025).

Additionally, the CDC Foundation supports fall prevention through educational programs and tools like the Falls Free CheckUp and the LIFE Tool, which help older adults assess their fall risk and create personalized prevention plans. These initiatives, backed by the CDC and other partners, aim to reduce fall-related injuries and hospitalizations by promoting proactive use of mobility aids and other safety measures (CDC Foundation, 2025).

Mobility Devices and Home Accessibility

Using mobility aids requires thoughtful home accessibility planning to ensure safety, independence, and ease of movement. A cane typically requires minimal adjustments, such as removing tripping hazards and ensuring good lighting. Walkers need wider pathways and stable, slip-resistant flooring to accommodate their broader base. Wheelchairs may demand extensive modifications, including widened doorways (typically 32 inches or more), ramp access, and accessible bathroom fixtures like roll-in (curbless) showers and grab bars.

Across all mobility aids, key considerations include, but are not limited to:

• **Accessible exterior and interior doorways:** For mobility devices, doorways should have at least 32 inches of clear opening or wheeled user space. The overall width and depth of the occupied mobility aid (including the person and the caregiver using the device) should be measured to ensure sufficient doorways and turning spaces.
• **Clear and wide pathways:** Ensure hallways and rooms are free of clutter and wide enough to accommodate walkers and wheelchairs.
• **Secure handrails and grab bars:** Install these in bathrooms, staircases, and other areas where extra support is needed.

- **Slip-resistant flooring:** Use slip-resistant surfaces to prevent falls, especially in bathrooms and kitchens.
- **Proper lighting:** Bright, even lighting helps users navigate safely, especially in stairways and entryways.
- **Accessible furniture and storage:** Arrange furniture to allow easy movement and keep frequently used items within reach. Frequently used items should be within easy reach and not too far outside of normal arms reach or outside the individual's base of support.
- **Threshold ramps and level transitions:** Eliminate steps or high thresholds that can impede movement or pose tripping hazards. For wheeled mobility devices, thresholds and floor transitions should be flush or not more than 1/4in. rise.
- **Modular (aluminum) ramp:** Modular ramps are low-maintenance. They should have a level landing with the door threshold and a ramp run that is 12 feet long for every 1 inch of rise (slope 1:12).
- **Smart home features:** Consider voice-activated lights, automated doors, smart appliances, or adjustable-height counters and tabletops for added convenience and safety.

Caregiver Considerations

Caregiver considerations must include ensuring adequate space in the home for both the mobility aid and the caregiver to operate safely and efficiently, especially when the individual requires extensive assistance with daily activities. This means:

- **Room for maneuvering:** Hallways, doorways, and living spaces should be wide enough to accommodate both the mobility device and the caregiver, allowing for smooth movement and positioning.
- **Transfer zones:** Areas around beds, toilets, and chairs should have enough clearance for safe transfers, whether using a gait belt, lift, or manual support.

- **Accessible layout:** Furniture should be arranged to avoid tight corners or obstacles, and essential items should be within reach to reduce unnecessary movement.
- **Emergency access:** Caregivers need to be able to quickly and safely reach the individual in case of a fall or medical emergency.
- **Storage and charging:** If using powered mobility aids, space for charging stations and secure storage is essential.

For additional strategies on adapting the home environment to support both caregiver and mobility needs, see Chapters 1, 3, 6, and 8.

Navigating Your Community Environments

Using mobility aids in the community opens a world of possibilities for older adults, allowing them to stay connected, active, and engaged in everyday life. Whether it is a trip to the park, a visit to a local café, or attending a family gathering, these outings can be deeply meaningful, but they do require some thoughtful planning to make sure everything goes smoothly.

The first step is choosing a destination that is truly accessible. That means looking for places with ramps, wide doorways, smooth walkways, and restrooms that accommodate mobility devices. It is also helpful to find spots with comfortable seating and quiet areas for rest, especially if the environment tends to be busy or crowded.

Transportation is another important piece of the puzzle. Whether you are using a personal vehicle or public transit, it is essential to make sure the mobility aid can be safely transported and that transfers in and out of the vehicle are manageable. Weather plays a role too. Extreme heat, rain, or icy conditions can affect both comfort and safety, so it is good to plan accordingly.

Before heading out, take a moment to check the mobility aid. Ensure brakes, wheels, and accessories like cushions or bags are in good shape. Caregivers should be ready to assist with navigation, transfers, and any personal needs, and it helps if they're familiar with how the device works and the individual's specific preferences or limitations.

It's also wise to pack a few essentials: medications, identification, a phone, and emergency contact information. Adding extra time for transitions and breaks can make the outing feel relaxed and enjoyable. Choosing locations with shaded areas and clear signage adds to the comfort and ease of the experience.

Ultimately, with a little preparation and care, community outings can be joyful and empowering for older adults using mobility aids, offering not just physical movement, but meaningful connection and independence.

Transporting Your Mobility Device

Transporting a mobility device for an outing is more than just logistics, it's about creating a smooth, safe, and enjoyable experience. Start by considering the type and size of the mobility aid. Some devices fold easily and fit into a car trunk, while others, especially powered wheelchairs or scooters, may need a vehicle with a lift. It is important to make sure there's enough room not just for the device, but also for the person using it and anyone helping with transfers.

Mobility aids are transported in the community in various ways depending on the type of aid, the individual's needs, and the available community infrastructure.

Personal Vehicles

- Trunk or backseat storage: Foldable walkers, canes, and manual wheelchairs can often be stored in a car.
- Vehicle-mounted carriers: External carriers for scooters or power chairs. For SUVs and vans, there are exterior and interior lift systems available.

Wheelchair-accessible vans: Equipped with ramps and lifts and securement systems.

Public Transportation

- Buses and trains: Many are equipped with ramps, lifts, and designated spaces for mobility aids.
- Paratransit services: Specialized transport for individuals with disabilities, often door-to-door.
- Accessible taxis and ride-shares: Some services offer vehicles with ramps or lifts.

Community Support Services

- Nonprofits and adult day centers: May offer transport services or loaner mobility aids.
- Medical transport companies: Provide professional transport for individuals with mobility challenges.

Air and Long-Distance Travel

- Airlines: Allow mobility aids to be checked or brought onboard; some offer aisle chairs.
- Trains and buses: Long-distance services often accommodate mobility aids with advance notice.

Transporting mobility aids have some challenges that can affect individuals, their caregivers, or transport provider. These challenges vary depending on the type of aid, the environment, and the mode of transportation.

One of the most common challenges is simply the physical nature of the equipment. Many mobility aids, especially power wheelchairs and scooters, are large, heavy, and not easily foldable. This can make it difficult to fit them into standard vehicles or navigate tight spaces, especially in older buildings or public transport systems that weren't designed with accessibility in mind.

While progress has been made, not all public transportation options are equipped to handle mobility aids comfortably or safely. Inconsistent infrastructure, like missing ramps, narrow doorways, or uneven sidewalks, can turn a simple outing into a stressful ordeal. Even when accessible options exist, they may be limited in availability or require advance planning, which can restrict spontaneity and independence.

Safety is also a concern. Improperly secured mobility aids during transport can pose risks. And unfortunately, damage during handling is not uncommon, especially when aids are stored in cargo holds or transferred frequently. These tools are essential to daily life, so any damage can be deeply disruptive.

Cost and availability of specialized transport services can be another barrier. Accessible vehicles and professional transport services often come with a high price tag, and not all insurance plans or public programs cover them. This can leave individuals and families juggling financial strain alongside logistical challenges.

Lastly, there's the emotional impact. Relying on others for transportation or facing repeated obstacles can lead to feelings of isolation or frustration.

It is not just about getting from point A to point B, it is about maintaining dignity, independence, and connection to your community.

Funding Mobility Aids

Funding mobility aids is an important aspect of promoting independence, safety, and quality of life as they age. Many older adults face financial barriers when trying to access essential devices like walkers, wheelchairs, and scooters, which can significantly impact their ability to move freely and participate in daily activities. Programs such as Medicare, Medicaid, supplemental insurances, and managed care plans fund partial coverage, but eligibility and benefits can vary widely, leaving gaps in support.

For example, traditional Medicare Part B typically covers 80% of the approved cost for durable medical equipment (DME) for individuals who meet the Medicare coverage criteria, including mobility aids like walkers, wheelchairs, and scooters. However, the remaining 20% of the cost is the patient's responsibility unless they have secondary or supplemental insurance. These additional insurance plans often cover the remaining 20%, significantly reducing out-of-pocket expenses for older adults. It's important for Medicare beneficiaries to ensure that both their doctor and the equipment supplier are enrolled in Medicare to receive full benefits. Understanding this coverage structure helps older adults and caregivers plan financially and access the mobility aids they need without undue burden.

Nonprofit organizations, community grants, and local government initiatives often play a vital role in bridging these gaps, providing financial assistance or donated equipment to those in need. Expanding awareness and access to these funding sources is essential to ensure that all older adults can benefit from the mobility aids that help them live with dignity and autonomy.

Alternative funding sources, including their eligibility and benefits, may differ state by state. These include, but are not limited to:

Veterans Affairs (VA) Benefits

• Veterans may be eligible for mobility aids through the VA, which often provides full coverage for durable medical equipment (DME) if it's deemed medically necessary.

State Assistive Technology Programs

• Many states have programs that offer loans, grants, or equipment lending libraries to help residents access assistive devices.

Area Agencies on Aging (AAA)

• Local AAAs often have information on community resources, grants, and programs that support older adults in obtaining mobility aids.

Charitable Organizations and Foundations

• Groups like the Muscular Dystrophy Association, United Way, and Lions Clubs may offer assistance or donated equipment.

Final Thoughts

As we reflect on the journey of aging, it becomes clear that mobility is more than just movement, it is a gateway to independence, dignity, and joy. "Aging in Motion: Rolling into the Golden Years" reminds us that embracing mobility aids is not a concession, but a celebration of resilience and adaptability. Mobility devices, when thoughtfully integrated into our homes and communities, become enablers of freedom, allowing us to continue exploring, connecting, and thriving.

Creating environments that support mobility is a shared responsibility. It is one that calls for innovation, empathy, and inclusive design. When we prioritize accessibility and usability, we foster a society where aging is not feared but embraced, where every step, roll, or glide is a testament to a life well-lived and still full of promise. Let us continue to champion mobility as a cornerstone of graceful aging, ensuring that the golden years truly shine with possibility, purpose, and motion.

[9]

Resilient by Design: Emergency Planning for Aging Communities

By
Felicia Saraceno

We all understand the importance of having an emergency plan. We're reminded of it annually, especially with news headlines about hurricane season, hailstorms, and tornadoes. Yet, many of us still overlook these warnings, assuming we have some vague backup plan. This complacency, combined with our rapidly growing aging population, highlights the critical need to prepare and protect older adults, particularly those living alone or without a robust support network.

The Silver Lining: Senior Living Communities

Fortunately, there's a significant advantage: senior living communities are uniquely positioned to make a difference. These communities help mitigate the risks many older adults face during crises, from social isolation and health issues to mobility challenges, nutritional needs, medication management, and lack of transportation. They offer built-in support systems, healthcare coordination, and trained teams ready to assist at every turn.

Across the United States, over 2 million older adults reside in approximately 31,000 senior living communities. Which includes independent living, assisted living, memory care, long term care facilities such as skilled nursing facilities and continuing care retirement communities (CCRC). This means senior living providers play a crucial role in ensuring older adults' safety. Their entire team must be trained for all types of emergencies and know when to evacuate or when it's safer to shelter in place. Did you know many senior living communities will set up a respite stay during your weather season? Which includes a furnished room with a commitment stay of typically thirty days in which you have all the same benefits residents residing in their community have for a short-term stay. This provides so many older adults and their families with peace of mind during high season natural disasters can strike.

A "Whole Community" Approach to Emergency Preparedness

The Administration for Community Living advocates for a "whole community" approach to emergency preparedness. This includes collaboration with local hospitals, home care providers, home health care, Area Agencies on Aging, Long-Term Care Ombudsman Programs, Aging and Disability Resource Centers, and other vital organizations. This collaborative effort is crucial because nearly half of adults over 65 live with two or more chronic conditions, such as heart disease, diabetes, or dementia, which significantly increase their vulnerability during any crisis.

The Increasing Frequency of Disasters

According to Climate.gov, every State in the U.S. has experienced a federally declared state of emergency or a major disaster since 2005. In fact, 2023 saw a historic high of 28 weather and climate disasters in the U.S. Over the last ten years (2015-2024), the U.S. has been impacted by 190 separate billion-dollar disasters that have killed more than 6,300 people (direct and indirect fatalities) and cost ~$1.4 trillion in damage.

Given these statistics, having a personal emergency plan is no longer optional—it's crucial. Many local communities offer support systems for this, and we owe it to ourselves and our loved ones to ensure everyone is prepared when the time comes.

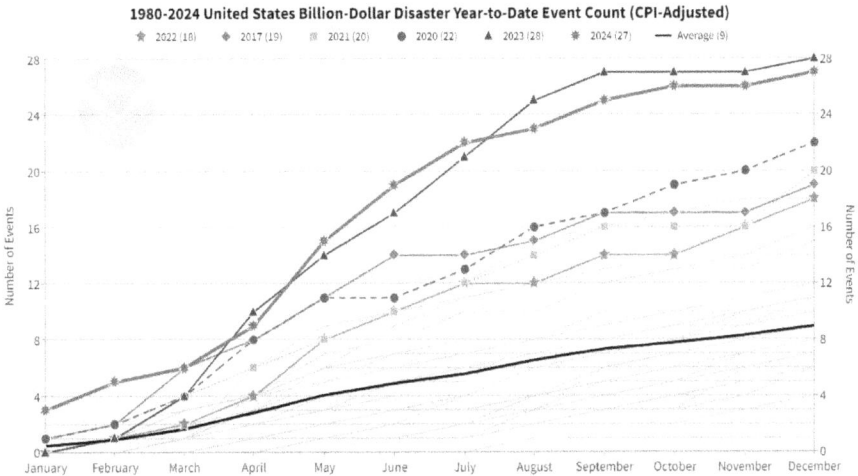

1980-2024 United States Billion-Dollar Disaster Year-to-Date Event Count (CPI-Adjusted)

My Background and Why This Matters

My name is Felicia Saraceno, and my current role involves assisting older adults in navigating the process of rightsizing their homes, taking a look at their capital gains impact, figure out how to pay for their care as they age and potentially moving into what I like to call their "forever home," which could be a senior living community. For the past four years, I've served as president of Naples Interagency, a local nonprofit supporting senior services and raising scholarship funds for healthcare students who serve the older population. I'm also the co-founder of Productive Aging Collective, a coaching platform for real estate agents who assist older adults in rightsizing their properties nationwide and take a financial look at their capital gains and provide much needed guidance of how to spend down for care needs as one ages in place.

Prior to these roles, my extensive experience in senior living included serving as an executive director and sales director, during which time I helped more than 360 older adults transition into their next chapter of life or "forever home." In senior living, our team annually reviewed the emergency preparedness plan to ensure our community was in peak condition, ready to face any challenges and partnered with local emergency support services to conduct hands-on training for the entire team. When your role involves ensuring the safety of a senior living community that houses over a hundred residents and a hundred employees, it is imperative that every aspect of your emergency plan is ready to be implemented at a moment's notice.

Getting Prepared, No Matter Where You Live

Let's explore how you can get prepared, regardless of your location in our beautiful country. Weather often dictates the majority of our emergency plans. Whether it's a blizzard, a nor'easter, an earthquake, a hailstorm, a tornado, a dreaded hurricane, a car accident that strikes an electrical pole, or even an electrical blackout, disasters typically strike with little warning. When they do, it's time to implement the plan you already have in place!

Crafting Your Plan

Developing your plan hinges on a few key factors: the amount of storage you have for supplies, who will be with you, and your local climate. It is ideal to create a formalized plan and share it with your loved ones. When disaster strikes, cell phones may be down, and many Americans no longer have landlines. Cell phone lines may be jammed or inoperable, and internet connections can also be disrupted. If your electrical power goes out, do you have a backup generator? Many older adults I have worked with made arrangements to stay with friends out of town, some have proactively moved into a senior living community to avoid annual emergency seasons, and others have arranged for short-term "respite stays" during hurricane or winter seasons. Whatever plan you decide on, ensuring you have all the necessary supplies is essential.

The plan we provide to our clients is adaptable for any geographical location. For example, our group of loved ones maintains a six-month supply of food, a one-month supply of bottled water, water filter devices, including food supplies for our family fur babies if they have pets. We also know which loved ones we'll connect with to ride out the emergency. When Hurricane Irma struck Southwest Florida, our home lost power for almost nine days. Gas for our generator lasted about half that time, and we nearly ran out of food in our brand-new house. It was quite an introduction to hurricane season as brand-new Floridians who just relocated from the Northeast.

How to Create Your Plan

Plan A: Utilize Your Storage Space

First, assess your storage areas and identify how you can maximize their use. Key items to have on hand include:

- A 5-10-day supply of water
- Food supplies (we prefer a six-month supply emergency food kit)
- Water filter devices (like "life straws" that convert any water into drinkable water)
- Daily medications and a detailed list of them
- Vitamins
- Comprehensive first aid kit
- Toiletries
- Candles
- Fuel
- Generators and battery backups
- Battery-operated radio and clock

- Compass
- Pet supplies
- Disposable kitchenware
- List of local emergency support contacts, including phone numbers
- Paper maps with a pre-planned route to another safe location, if needed
- Extra master set of keys for your home and vehicles
- Other electronic key household data
- Flares
- Toilet paper and paper towels
- Most importantly, your Advanced Directive and Power of Attorney (POA) paperwork.

NOTE: We even have a comprehensive checklist in the documents and reference area to ensure you have everything you need!

Plan B: Connect with Your Network

If you don't have enough storage space for all these items, start thinking about Plan B: Who can you connect with and who can house you during an emergency or disaster? Make these arrangements in advance and always have a backup plan in place as well.

After the Storm: Getting Back to Normal

Looking ahead to a period after a storm, disaster, or power outage, your focus always shifts to recovery mode and getting back to normal. What to consider? Assess property damage, what is open for fuel, restaurants, grocery stores and so on. Reconnecting with these types of services or businesses can provide a sense of security and normalcy. This is where your emergency radio can come in handy if power has not been restored or cell phone service is still spotty.

Post-Storm Recovery Checklist – Who to Contact:
- Local Emergency Management Office: for disaster updates, shelter info, and recovery resources
- County Health Department: for health alerts, water safety, and medical resources
- Local Power & Utility Companies: to report outages or damage to power lines, gas, or water
- 911 (for Emergencies) and Non-Emergency Police Line: for urgent and non-urgent safety concerns
- FEMA or Local Disaster Recovery Centers: for federal aid and support services
- Senior Services or Area Agency on Aging: for additional support specific to older adults
- Insurance Providers: to start claims for property damage or loss
- Family Emergency Contacts: to update loved ones on status and next steps

A Call to Action

No matter your age or living situation, taking the time to prepare now can make all the difference when a crisis strikes. Let's work together as a community to ensure the safety and well-being of our older adults, empowering them to age in place with confidence and security. Your proactive steps today will create a safer tomorrow for yourself and your loved ones.

Pillar 3:
Finances

[10]

Medicare: Does It Have to Be So Confusing?

By
James Donnelly

Introduction

When I was first introduced to Medicare, I thought it was simple. I figured it was just health insurance for older adults when they turned age 65. That was it. Straightforward, right?

Well, not exactly.

My introduction came the hard way. My grandmother had taken a fall, had hip surgery, and was moved into a rehab facility. Out of nowhere, my family called me in a panic: *"Her insurance isn't covering this! Someone switched her plan! What do we do?"* And of course, since I was the "insurance guy," they all assumed I had the answers.

Truth was, I didn't. I wasn't the Medicare guy then. I had to dive headfirst into a maze of terms, rules, penalties, exceptions, and choices that felt like they were written in another language. Fast forward seven years later, and now I spend my days breaking down Medicare as simply as possible for families like mine.

Because here's the truth: Medicare is confusing - but it doesn't have to be.

Who Is Eligible for Medicare?

Most people become eligible at age 65 if they or their spouse worked at least 40 quarters - that's 10 years - paying Medicare taxes.

But what if you didn't work the full 40 quarters? Medicare is still available to you, but you'll have to pay a premium for Part A (hospital coverage). The fewer quarters you worked, the higher your premium.

And here's something most people don't know: you don't have to be age 65. If you've been on Social Security Disability Insurance for 24 months, you qualify. If you've been diagnosed with ALS (Lou Gehrig's disease) or end-stage renal disease, you qualify sooner.

Case Story – Candice's Surprise

Candice, age 28, received disability benefits for two years due to a very bad car accident. She assumed Medicare was only for people over age 65 and didn't realize she qualified early. When we reviewed her situation, she was shocked to learn she could sign up right away - and relieved that she didn't have to struggle with costly marketplace coverage anymore.

Do You Have to Apply for Medicare?

There's a common belief that everyone automatically must enroll in Medicare at age 65 and I run into this at a lot of my Medicare seminars. Adults turning age 65 run to enroll in Part A and/or B. The truth is, this only has to be done 50% of the time.

If you're still working and covered under an employer group health plan with more than 20 employees, you don't have to sign up right away. You can delay Medicare without a penalty.

But if you're not working, or you're working for a small employer (fewer than 20 employees), then yes - you must sign up.

Even if you can delay, it's worth doing a review. Healthcare costs are rising, and sometimes Medicare ends up being the more affordable and comprehensive option.

Case Story – Tom's Dilemma

Tom turned age 65 while still working for a company with fewer than 20 employees. He thought he could keep his work insurance, but because the company was small, Medicare was supposed to be his primary insurance. He didn't sign up. The result? His employer's plan refused claims that Medicare should have covered. Tom ended up with a stack of unpaid medical bills. A quick consultation before his birthday could have prevented the whole mess.

How Do You Sign Up?

Enrolling in Medicare isn't automatic for everyone. You've got a few options:

• Call Social Security and set up a phone appointment.
• Go into your local Social Security office.
• Apply online through the Social Security website.
• Or, work with a licensed broker who can guide you through it.

Your Initial Enrollment Period (IEP) is three months before your 65th birthday, the month of, and three months after. Miss it, and you may face delays and penalties.

Case Story – Linda's Delay

Linda decided she'd "deal with Medicare later" after retiring. By the time she came to me, she was outside her enrollment window. She had to wait months for coverage to start, and she was hit with a Part B penalty that will stick with her forever. She told me, *"If I had known how serious this was, I never would've put it off."*

The Penalty Box

If you don't enroll when you're supposed to, you'll face lifetime penalties:

• Part B (medical insurance): 10% penalty for every year you delay.
• Part D (prescription drugs): 1% penalty for every month you delay.

And these penalties don't go away. They follow you for life.

Case Story – My Mother-In-Law Penalty

My mother-in-law retired at age 65 but didn't think she needed Part D drug coverage since she wasn't taking any medications. When she finally signed up at age 75, she was hit with a 100% lifetime penalty on her drug plan premium. Her words to me: *"I thought I was saving money. Instead, I locked myself into paying more for the rest of my life."*

Breaking Down Medicare Parts A, B, C, and D

Part A: Hospital insurance covering inpatient stays, skilled nursing, hospice, some home health. Premium-free if you worked 40 quarters.

Part B: Medical insurance covering doctors, outpatient services, preventive care. Comes with a monthly premium and 20% cost-sharing.

Part C (Medicare Advantage): Private plans bundling A, B, and usually D, plus extras like dental, vision, and hearing. Lower premiums but network restrictions.

Part D: Prescription drug coverage. Standalone or bundled in Medicare Advantage. Premiums vary and penalties apply if you delay.

Medigap Versus Medicare Advantage

You've got two main paths:

1. Original Medicare + Medigap + Part D: higher monthly premium, but fewer surprises and broad doctor access.

2. Medicare Advantage: lower upfront premiums, more copays, extras included, but network restrictions.

There's no one-size-fits-all choice. It depends on health, finances, and lifestyle.

Case Story – My Parents

Mom wanted predictability. She chose Medigap and paid more each month but never worried about surprise bills. Dad, on the other hand, was healthy and wanted low monthly costs. He went with Medicare Advantage and saved money - until he had surgery and saw the copays add up.

Enrollment Periods You Need to Know

Initial Enrollment Period (IEP): Around your 65th birthday.
Special Enrollment Periods (SEPs): Triggered by retirement, loss of coverage, or moving.
Annual Enrollment Period (AEP): October 15 – December 7 each year.

Open Enrollment Period (OEP): January 1 – March 31 for Medicare Advantage changes.

Common Mistakes People Make

Some of the biggest mistakes include:
1. Assuming you don't need to sign up.
2. Listening to friends instead of professionals. (Locker room talk)
3. Skipping Part D because you "don't take medications."
4. Not reviewing plans annually.
5. Forgetting about network restrictions.

Case Story – The "Neighbor Expert"

One of my clients, Fran, signed up for the same Medicare Advantage plan as her neighbor because "it worked great for him." The problem was Fran's prescriptions weren't on the plan's formulary, and his doctor wasn't in-network. What works for one person doesn't always work for another.

Why Annual Reviews Are Essential

Medicare doesn't stay the same: plans change every year, premiums rise, formularies are updated, and doctors move in and out of networks.

I had one client, Theresa, who didn't review her plan for three years. She came to me after realizing one of her prescriptions was no longer covered, and she had spent thousands out-of-pocket. One quick review would've prevented it.

A Quick Word on Health Insurance (for the Spouse "Left Behind")

Working with Medicare recipients, I quickly realized there was always one person left out of the equation: the spouse who wasn't yet age 65. Medicare was great for the eligible partner, but what about the other half of the couple?

In the beginning, I worked through the federal exchange and state exchanges to find coverage for these younger spouses. But there weren't many options outside of the exchange for private insurance or qualified health plans.

So, I went on a relentless search. Trust me, no door was left unopened. Over time, I discovered there actually are several options:

• Exchange-based plans ("Obamacare")
• Union and association plans
• Health-sharing accounts

Here's the key: health insurance under age 65 is very different from Medicare. Formularies, drug prices, and benefits can look nothing alike.

And then you've got group health insurance versus individual health insurance. That's a whole different ballgame. With group plans, you often see lower costs and better benefits because the risk is shared among many employees. With individual plans, everything comes down to your age, your health, and your area.

Let's talk about the basics:

• **Copayment:** what you pay at the doctor's office or pharmacy each visit.
• **Deductible:** what you pay out-of-pocket each year before insurance kicks in.
• **Out-of-pocket maximum:** the most you'll pay in a year before insurance covers 100%.

And here's the kicker: the lower your deductible, copayment, and out-of-pocket maximum, the higher your premium will be. Insurance is always about trade-offs. Everything is relative.

Tying It Back to Medicare

So, how does this tie into Medicare?

Simple. Families don't live in silos. When one spouse goes on Medicare, the other may still need individual or group coverage. Understanding both sides of the fence - health insurance under age 65 and Medicare over age 65 - allows me to guide families through every stage of life's transitions.

Because whether you're dealing with an employer plan, an exchange plan, health-sharing, or Medicare itself, the principles are the same: know your options, know your costs, and make sure your coverage works for you.

At the end of the day, Medicare is just one piece of a bigger puzzle. And my job is to make sure every piece fits.

When my grandmother's situation first threw me into the Medicare world, I never imagined I'd make it my career. But that experience showed me how important it is for families to have someone who can translate this complicated system into plain English.

Medicare is confusing, yes. But it doesn't have to be. With the right knowledge and the right guidance, you can avoid penalties, save money, and make sure you're protected.

At the end of the day, Medicare isn't just about insurance - it's about peace of mind. And that's something everyone deserves.

[11]

LTC-Life Settlements: Cashing Out Life Insurance Policies to Age in Place

By
Chris Orestis

Senior care providers frequently encounter clients who while in the process of preparing for the transition to senior living and long-term care still own a life insurance policy. It is little wonder why because today there are over 260 million in-force life insurance policies in the U.S. with over $20 trillion of in-force death benefit. Compare that to the 7.5 million of in-force long-term care insurance policies and you may begin to realize that this is a massive untapped pool of assets that can be cashed out to help people pay for their care needs through a financial option known as an LTC-Life Settlement.

What is a Life Insurance Policy Settlement

Life settlements are simply enough the sale of a life insurance policy by the original owner to a third-party who will pay the owner a percentage of the death benefit while they are still alive. A life settlement transaction involves no costs for the seller of the policy, takes 60-90 days to complete, and once the ownership of the policy is transferred the original owner is no longer responsible for premium payments. Life settlements are a way to cash out a life insurance policy later in life while still alive instead of abandoning it after years of premium payments. It can also be a tax-advantaged transaction based on the severity of health impairments of the insured and total premiums paid into the policy.

This is a unique financial option because it rewards the owner of life insurance policies as they get older and sicker with increasing settlement value for their policy. Someone else buys, or "settles," the policy and pays the owner a lump-sum less than the full death benefit. The new owner takes over the premium payments until they collect the death benefit in the future upon the passing of the insured. The shorter the time frame that the new owner actuarially calculates they will wait to collect the death benefit, the more they will pay to the original owner to settle the policy. Buyers of policies are most often large, regulated financial institutions such as investment banks, hedge funds and investment groups who work through companies licensed to transact life settlements.

LTC-Life Settlements for Aging in Place and Senior Care

LTC-Life Settlements, established in 2007 and available in all 50 states, is a valuable financial solution for older adults who require long-term care services. It provides immediate funding for a wide range of care options, including home care, assisted living, skilled nursing care, memory care, and hospice. Unlike traditional long-term care insurance, annuities, or loans, LTC-Life Settlement offers a unique advantage by eliminating wait periods and claims processes. Once the policy is settled, payments for care can begin immediately, giving older adults total control to address their evolving care needs without bureaucratic delays.

Additionally, LTC-Life Settlement offers significant tax benefits for policyholders diagnosed with chronic or terminal conditions. For those meeting specific medical criteria—such as needing assistance with two or more Activities of Daily Living (ADLs) or having a life expectancy of two years or less—funds can be received tax-free.* These funds are private pay, providing a delay in the need for Medicaid and ensuring that payments made toward care count as part of a Medicaid-qualified spend-down. This flexibility and accessibility make LTC-Life Settlement an essential option for older adults seeking financial security and control over their long-term care needs.

How a Life Settlement Works

A life settlement is the sale of a life insurance policy by the policy holder while still alive for a percentage of the in-force death benefit in the form of valuable consideration such as lump-sum cash, LTC benefits, ongoing, reduced death benefits, or other financial instrument such as an annuity. It is the legal right of every life insurance policy owner to be able to sell their policy, like any other asset, to a new owner who will take over the premium payments and then collect the death benefit years later.

Most often, a Life Settlement is for adults over the age of 65 with a life insurance policy above $100,000 of face value. The value of a Life Settlement is based on "reverse underwriting' so the older and sicker a person is, the more they will get from a life Settlement. Someone too young and healthy will not qualify for a Life Settlement. The typical age range for a life settlement is 75-92, but younger or older applicants can qualify based on the severity of their health-related impairments, and the typical life expectancy range for a qualified candidate is sub-ten years. People experiencing declining health, chronic conditions needing long-term care, and possibly terminal diagnosis are appropriate candidates for a life settlement.

Any type of in-force life insurance could potentially qualify for a life settlement. Term Life, Universal Life, and Whole Life policies with $100,000 or more of death benefit are all eligible. The process of a Life Settlement takes about 60-90 days, and thousands of transactions are completed every year. Policy owners tend to receive between 10%-50% (industry average 22.5%) of the face value by transferring the ownership of their policy through the insurance company to the new owner. There are no fees of any type for a policy owner using a life settlement.

Life Insurance in Legally Recognized as an Asset

The landmark Supreme Court case *Grigsby v. Russell* (1911) established that life insurance policies are legally recognized as property, granting policy owners the right to sell their policies to third parties. Justice Oliver Wendell Holmes affirmed that life insurance possesses all the attributes of personal property, equating it to assets like real estate or stocks. Today, life insurance policies are one of the most valuable and stable assets a person can own because the death benefit is guaranteed for as long as the premiums are paid. But some policy holders may find that they no longer need their policy and every owner can benefit from their legal right to sell off an unneeded or unwanted policy through a life settlement.

Most people don't realize that a life insurance policy is personal property just like their home and that it has fair-market value while they are alive, and too often abandon their policy as older adults. The problem is that not enough policy owners are aware of this unique financial option designed specifically to benefit them while they are still alive. Annual insurance industry numbers show that as many as 9 out of 10 life insurance policies are in danger of being lapsed or surrendered by the owners. Hundreds of billions worth of life insurance is abandoned every year before paying out a death benefit. Unfortunately, lapsing a policy by stopping payments cancels it rendering it worthless and for policies that may have cash surrender value (CSV) a life settlement is often a better option than surrender because on average life settlements will pay out 5X-10X more than CSV.

On an annual basis, over $200 billion of life insurance is owned by older adults who are in danger of lapsing or surrendering a policy who could potentially sell their policy instead through a Life Settlement. But awareness about this financial option is growing from TV commercials similar to a reverse mortgage running constantly on TV, radio and online. Life Settlements have grown into a very mainstream and well-regulated financial vehicle with about $4.5 billion of Life Settlements done by policy owners every year.

Better Options for an Unneeded Policy

Life insurance policies have been legally recognized as assets for over 100 years and covey the same personal property ownership rights as assets such as real estate or stocks. In fact, think of a life insurance policy like a home. They are both personal property of the owner and they both have value. After years of mortgage payments, a homeowner would not abandon their property without selling it. The same is true for a life insurance policy. After years of premium payments, the owner should not abandon their asset without first seeking to obtain its fair market value. No one should ever lapse or surrender a life insurance policy without first finding out what the higher market value of that policy could be for them through a life settlement.

What are some of the options that a life policy owner could consider exchanging their death benefit for a new living benefit?

• A life insurance policy can be settled for a lump-sum cash payment that the policy owner can then use without any restrictions to address their financial needs. Instead of abandoning a policy after years of making premium payments, the owner could receive significant value, which often runs 5-10X greater than cash value if there is any, for their asset.

• A life insurance policy can be settled to pay for immediate need for senior living and long-term care services with no wait periods or claims to file. Funds from an LTC-Life Settlement can be tax-free for a policy owner medically diagnosed as chronic (2 ADL's or more) or terminal (2 years or less of life expectancy). The funds are private pay and will delay the need for Medicaid, but paid towards care they are recognized as a Medicaid qualified spend-down.*

• A life insurance policy can be settled for other financial vehicles such as an annuity. If a policy owner's concern is outliving their money, then enrolling in an annuity would be a solution to ensure a guaranteed lifetime income stream. This is a tax-advantaged option to help protect and manage funds to augment an older adults retirement income and help with the expensive costs of health and long-term care.

• A life insurance policy can be settled for a reduced, paid-up death benefit to continue financial protection for a family. This allows a policy owner who can no longer afford to pay premiums the chance to keep a portion of their death benefit without making any future premium payments. For a policy owner still in need of death benefit protection, this is an ideal option instead of lapsing or surrendering their policy after years premium payments.

Ideal candidates for a life settlement

Declining health is a key factor in determining eligibility and value for a life settlement. Qualifying for a Life Settlement is the opposite of qualifying to purchase insurance, and the value of a Life Settlement is based on "reverse underwriting' so the older and sicker a person is, the more they will get from a Life Settlement. Someone too young and healthy will not qualify for a Life Settlement. If someone would qualify to buy life or long-term care insurance, they would not qualify for a life settlement and vice versa. In fact, the older and sicker the insured life of the policy is, the higher percentage of the death benefit the policy owner will receive in "present-day value". This is important for older adults who are experiencing declining health and financial complications.

Typical Eligibility:

- In-force life insurance policy (Universal, Term, Whole) with a death benefit of $100,000 and above
- Older adult policy owners in declining health who are now looking for financial help with retirement and LTC
- Policies that are in danger of lapse or surrender and may be abandoned if action isn't taken
- LTC insurance policy owners on claim
- Underperforming UL policies
- Term life policies prior to conversion
- Policy owners considering partial surrender
- Policy owners looking for an "exit strategy" out of an unneeded policy (outlived the insurable interest, Key Man policy, lower than estate tax levels)

Consumer Protections

The life settlement market is considered an insurance transaction and regulated by state insurance departments. There is no federal uniformity to the transaction such as there is with banking or securities, so settlement valuations can vary from company to company. Consumer protections for the policy owner are strong with a number of regulatory requirements in place:

1. Selling a policy is a highly transparent transaction

Prior to the sale of a policy, the seller receives numerous consumer disclosures. In most states, this includes all offers, the gross vs. net amount of the offer, sales commissions, comparisons of sale price versus the policy surrender value and accelerated death benefit amount, names of purchasers, and more.

2. When considering selling a policy, owners are advised of alternatives

Life settlement companies are required to provide sellers with information about keeping their policies in force, including disclosing that an accelerated death benefit or policy loan might be a better option. In addition, in most states, settlement offers disclose the settlement amount as compared to any accelerated death benefit that might be available under the policy.

3. Sellers also receive disclosures of certain risks when selling a policy

While in most cases the financial benefits of selling a policy far outweigh surrendering it back to the insurance company, there are certain risks that must be disclosed, including tax consequences, a reduction in government benefits due to increased assets, or creditor debt reducing the net value of the transaction.

4. Consumers receive a state-approved informational brochure about selling their policy

To ensure sellers understand exactly what they are agreeing to and the benefits they will receive, most state laws require that brokers and buyers provide sellers with a state-approved brochure that defines the transaction, explains how it works, and provides them with the contact information of the state insurance regulator.

5. Sellers must be deemed competent to enter into a settlement contract

Even with clear information, older adults who experience changes in memory or thinking may still struggle with important financial decisions. As a result, most states require that the seller's personal physician provide a certificate of mental competence prior to a sale—a protection that is unprecedented and underscores the emphasis on consumer safeguards.

6. Policy beneficiaries provide consent prior to the sale

Prior to the sale of the policy, most purchasers in the life insurance secondary market require the beneficiaries named in the policy to consent to the sale. This protects buyers and sellers alike against the risk of future litigation. (NOTE: This is not statutorily required – and cannot be – but it is a widely adopted industry practice.)

7. Buyers of life insurance policies must be licensed by the state

Because of the important focus on protections for older adults, only companies that are licensed by the state insurance department where the seller lives can enter into a life settlement contract with that seller. Licensees are subject to background checks, are required to provide detailed business plans, and to submit and comply with stringent anti-fraud measures.

Conclusion

Life settlements are specifically designed to provide the maximum available value for the policy and address the unique financial and healthcare needs of older adults and people experiencing declining health. Taking advantage of the life settlement value of a life insurance policy for a qualified policy owner is a much better strategy than lapse or surrender. Once a policy has been settled, the value can be used to remain in control of aging in place and senior living requirements, increase income, estate preservation, delay liquidating investments and assets, and it can protect a family from being financially ruined by the high costs of long-term care.

Life insurance policies are one of the most valuable assets a person can own. They are also one of the most misunderstood and wasted. Anyone contemplating the lapse or surrender of a life insurance policy should always look into the potential value of a life settlement first. As older adults confront the realities of aging and the impact that retirement and health care will have on their finances; it is creative financial opportunities like Life Settlements that can make the difference between possibly running out of money with years left to live or living those years with comfort and security.

FAST FACTS

• There are no costs for a policy owner to transact a life settlement with the typical time to complete a settlement between 60-90 days.

• Any form of life insurance can qualify for a life settlement, including: Term Life, Universal Life, Whole Life, and Variable Life policies.

• The range for a life settlement payout can be a low of 5%-10% to as high as 50% or more of the death benefit. The industry average payout is 20%-25%.

• The older and more impaired the health of the insured, the higher the payout for a life settlement.

• LTC-Life Settlements can be a tax-free way to pay for health and long-term care costs as part of a Medicaid spend down.*

• There are over 260 million in-force life insurance policies in the United States with more than $20T of death benefit.

• 88% of life insurance policies are in danger of either being lapsed or surrendered.

• On an annual basis, as much as $200B of in-force death benefit is owned by older adults who may lapse or surrender their policy without realizing it has significant life settlement value.

- There is approximately $4.5B of life settlement transactions completed in the United States every year.

- Life settlements can be a tax-free transaction for people diagnosed with chronic or terminal conditions, and the amount received from a life settlement is tax-free up to what has been paid into the policy in premiums.*

- Life insurance policies are legally recognized as assets, and the owner of a policy has the same personal property ownership rights to sell their policy as they do with a home.

- A life settlement is valued by "reverse underwriting," so the older and sicker a person is the more value they will find through a life settlement. The acceptable life expectancy range for a life settlement is 2-10 years.

- The National Association of Insurance Commissioners (NAIC) released the *White Paper Private Market Options for Financing Long-Term Care* endorsing life settlements as a way to pay for long-term care and specifically cited the higher values found for the consumer through a life settlement than to lapse or surrender a policy.

CASE STUDIES

Case Study A
A Son Helps His Mother Move into Assisted Living Community

$100,000 death benefit

The applicant's son called to inquire about how to rescue a life insurance policy they were planning to abandon. His mother was unable to live at home alone any longer, and they were looking into Assisted Living but needed financial help. Their mother owned a $100,000 life insurance policy. He completed a Policy Review application and submitted it along with policy information, authorizations and medical records. Within 30 days, the application was approved, and the $2,000 monthly Long-Term Care Benefit payments began that same day. The family moved their mother into the Assisted Living community where she was hoping to reside with several of her friends and relatives. By adding $2,000 a month to what they already had available to pay for her care, instead of moving her into their home and trying to hire home health aides, they were able to move their mother into the community where they all wanted her to be.

• $35,000 Total LTC-Settlement
• $2,000 Monthly Payment x 18 months

Case Study B
Policy Owner About to Abandon a Term Policy Discovers It's a Tax-Free Way to Pay for Needed Home Based Skilled Long-Term Care

$500,000 convertible term life policy

The policy owner was about to abandon a life insurance policy because they couldn't afford the premiums. The policy owner was experiencing declining health and had just completed an extended skilled rehabilitation stay of 6 weeks. The agent contacted us to see if we could look for and possibly help them with an LTC-Life Settlement. We reviewed the case and analyzed the more recent rehab records and within a week we were able to determine that the policy owner would qualify to settle their policy. The family moved forward with the LTC-Life Settlement and was able to immediately enroll in a Long-Term Care Benefit Account. We were also able to help them access a selection of homecare companies to make sure the client would be receiving the best possible care—which they could now afford.

• $200,000 Total LTC-Settlement
• $5,000 Monthly Payment x 40 months

Case Study C
Policy Owner Settles Policy to Pay for Assisted Living Community Before Being Evicted

$400,000 Universal Life Policy

A policy owner with a $400,000 UL owned a life insurance policy running out of cash value and could not afford to make future premium payments. The policy owner was already a resident of an assisted living community and was running out of money. The size of the policy and his need to pay for health care services made the policy owner a perfect candidate to settle the policy to fund a tax-free Long-Term Care Benefit Account. After working with the assisted living community to analyze the health needs of the policy owner, it was determined they would be able to receive significant settlement value from their policy to start covering their monthly costs. Within 30 days, the policy was settled, and the tax-free funds were placed into their Long-Term Care Benefit Account, providing enough funds to cover the costs of the assisted living for the next 3 years.

• $175,000 Total LTC-Settlement
• $4,000 Monthly Payment x 35 months

Case Study D
Son Helps His Mother Convert Policy and Move into Assisted Living Before He Deployed for Afghanistan

$100,000 death benefit

A family was struggling with how they would pay for the costs of moving their mother into an assisted living community. Increasing the pressure was the fact that her son was going to be leaving for Afghanistan within 90 days for a tour of duty with the military. Their mother owned a $100,000 life insurance policy that was going to lapse if they did not immediately make an expensive premium payment. The family was trying to determine what their options with the policy might be, when the assisted living community suggested that they contact consider using an LTC-Life Settlement with their life insurance policy to fund a Long-Term Care Benefit Account. Before the policy could lapse, they completed to Policy Review and settlement process which allowed them to immediately move their mother into the community. There was still time for her son to help her move-in and get settled before he left for Afghanistan later that month.

• $39,000 Total LTC-Settlement
• $2,100 Monthly Payment x 19 months

LTC-life settlement review: Q&A

Q: What forms of long-term care qualify?
A: LTC-Life Settlements will pay any form of care: • Home Care • Assisted Living • Memory Care • Nursing Home • Hospice Care

Q: Is this like Long-Term Care Insurance
A: No, they are very different. A person who would qualify to settle their policy would be an automatic decline for any form of insurance coverage. Also, there are no wait periods, claims, or limitations on forms of care or the amount that can be spent on a monthly basis for care.

Q: Are there any fees or premiums to do an LTC-Life Settlement?
A: No, there are no fees of any kind for the policy owner. Once a policy is settled the funds are immediately available, and the enrollee is relieved of any responsibility to pay premiums.

Q: Is the enrollee exchanging the ownership of the life insurance policy?
A: Yes, the enrollee will exchange all ownership and beneficiary rights to the life insurance policy. The enrollee is no longer responsible for premium payments, and the policy is no longer considered an asset that will count against them for future Medicaid eligibility.

Q: How does a LTC-Life Settlement impact Medicaid eligibility?
A: The policy transaction is specifically designed to conform to the secondary market regulations that govern life settlements; and funds spent on care are a Medicaid qualified spend-down of the asset proceeds. By obtaining the fair market value for the life policy, and then spending the money to pay for senior living and long-term care services; the LTC-Life Settlement is a regulated financial transaction, and a Medicaid qualified spend down to help cover the costs of long-term care.

Q: Is the LTC-Life Settlement available today?
A: Yes, first introduced into the market in 2007, LTC-Life Settlements are available in all 50 states, enjoy tremendous support from political leaders across the country, is accepted by all forms of senior living and long-term care providers, and has been used to pay millions of dollars in senior care.

* The author and/or Retirement Genius does not provide tax or legal advice. Nothing herein should be construed as investment, insurance, securities, tax or legal advice. Consumers should consult with their own tax, legal and/or financial advisors before engaging in any transaction. The information contained herein does not provide any advice as to the value of securities or as to the advisability of investing in, purchasing, or selling securities or insurance products. Decisions based on this information are the sole responsibility of the reader. The information contained herein is not an offer to sell or a solicitation of an offer to buy any security or any investment or insurance product or service.

Pillar 4:
Transportation

[12]
Driver Safety: A Caregiver's Guide

By
Melanie Henry

Introduction

Let's face it - bringing up driving concerns with an aging loved one is never easy. In fact, research shows that most adult children would rather talk to their parents about funeral plans than have a conversation about giving up the car keys. That's how emotionally charged this subject can be. But if you're a caregiver and you've noticed changes, or you just have that gut feeling that something isn't quite right, it's time to start the conversation.

It seems that everyone I meet has a story. Most people have either experienced this firsthand or know someone who's had to face tough decisions around a loved one's driving. I've been there, too - more than once.

I'm originally from Sydney, Australia. Years ago, my dad who was in his early 60s was living with undiagnosed vascular dementia. He was physically active and outwardly healthy, but he smoked two packs of cigarettes a day and refused to quit. He didn't believe in doctors. Despite being in good physical shape, I started to notice small but worrying changes in his mood and his ability to complete everyday tasks. He was no longer the upbeat, funny, caring man I had always known. His joy in life had faded. He stopped seeing his grandsons and spent most of his time alone, watching TV.

We initially assumed it was grief. Our mother, his wife of over 45 years, had recently passed away following a brief and devastating battle with stage 4 colon cancer. But something more was happening. The only activity my dad still enjoyed was driving to antique stores to search for a hidden treasure.

He still refused to see a doctor, and his decline continued. I often sat in my car after visiting him, windows rolled up, crying or screaming out of sheer frustration. I didn't know what was going on, and I didn't know what to do. His situation wasn't considered severe enough by the hospital's Adult Protective Services team, and he was adamant that he wasn't leaving his home. I became the "bad guy" in his eyes because I wanted him to sell the house and move into a long-term care community where he'd be safer. My sister and I weren't on the same page. She lived in a separate unit behind his home and wanted things to stay as they were. Like many of you reading this, I was in the thick of it.

This all happened years before I entered the field of driver evaluation and instruction. At the time, I was working in child protection, focused on criminal child abuse investigations. Like so many others, I had no idea driving evaluations even existed - let alone that there were resources available. Looking back, what a difference that knowledge would have made. My dad continued to drive right up until the day he entered a long-term care community. It's honestly a miracle that he didn't hurt himself or someone else.

While all of this was unfolding, I was also preparing to move to California with my American husband and our two boys - a heart-wrenching decision we made to give our growing sons the opportunity to pursue a U.S. college education.

Years later, while working as a Transportation Coordinator for a volunteer driver medical ride program in the Tri-Valley area of the San Francisco Bay Area, I had my "aha" moment. Some of our clients no longer drove to their medical appointments but were still driving to the grocery store. I kept asking myself: *How do we know they're still safe to drive? Who's evaluating that?*

Our office was located inside an adult day center, and nearly every week we witnessed incidents in the parking lot—cars left running while the driver was inside playing cards or having lunch, drivers hitting the gas instead of the brake and jumping the wheel stop, or even minor collisions in the parking lot and sadly, we heard about some clients totaling their vehicles.

That's when I realized the urgent need for an independent driving assessment center—somewhere families could turn to for clarity, guidance, and support.

This chapter is for you.

The caregiver. The spouse. The adult child. The concerned family member, friend, or support person who's worried about someone they love but isn't sure how to begin, or where to turn.

In the pages ahead, I'll explore why driving is so meaningful for older adults, how to recognize the warning signs, and how to approach this difficult topic with empathy and confidence. I'll also equip you with practical strategies, conversation tips, and resources to help guide your loved one through the transition.

You're not alone. And this work matters, more than you know.

Why Driving Is More Than Just a Ride

In the U.S., driving is synonymous with independence. It gives us the freedom to come and go, stay connected, and make our own decisions. For older adults, this sense of control becomes even more significant. Losing the ability to drive often feels like losing a part of oneself - freedom, identity, lifestyle and losing control over another aspect of life. For some, they are so scared and feel very threatened that their adult children are going to make even more decisions about their life. No wonder it's such a touchy subject.

As a caregiver, you might feel stuck between keeping your loved one safe and not wanting to damage your relationship. You're not alone. Many families avoid "the talk" because they fear anger, denial, or even threats of disownment. But waiting can lead to greater risks, not only for your loved one, but for others on the road. There is also potential liability and risk to think about. Especially if your loved one lives in a litigious state like California.

Why Driving Concerns Are So Hard to Talk About

Driving is deeply personal. For many older adults, it's tied to a lifetime of experience and pride. They often believe they are still good drivers, after all, they've been doing it for many decades. It's common to hear, "I'm fine. I only drive a few miles to the store." But the truth is, a cognitively unsafe driver is a risk whether they drive one mile or ten.

Medical conditions that impact mental abilities, medications that have side effects, the situation becomes even more complex. Individuals with cognitive impairment often lack awareness and insight and are genuinely surprised when concerns are raised. That's why this conversation can't wait until something serious happens.

What Research Tells Us

The good news? Statistically, older adults are among the safest drivers. They tend to drive fewer miles and often avoid risky situations like night driving, freeway travel, and rush hour. Modern cars with advanced safety features such as blind spot monitoring, lane control, brake assist, back up cameras and so on, also help.

This year, a quarter of all U.S. drivers will be 65 years or older. Many will keep their licenses longer, even as their health changes.

According to AAA and the American Medical Association, drivers over 85 have a per-mile fatality rate nine times higher than drivers aged 25 to 69. This is not because of driving more miles or having more collisions, but because of the frailty of the human body as we age.
Drivers with cognitive impairment are over three times as likely to cause a crash.

According to the Alzheimer's Association there are over 7.2 million Americans living with dementia. They estimate 30–40% are driving. That's roughly 2.1 to 2.8 million individuals driving with dementia. The challenge is that many individuals who have dementia are undiagnosed. Many try to hide the cognitive changes occurring and many will not talk with their families or friends about what they are experiencing.

On top of this, the research tells us that less than 20% of patients discuss driving with their physician because they fear their driver license will be suspended or revoked. In addition, many physicians are not having these conversations with their patients until there is a concern. On top of it all, many physicians do not know about driver assessment services and resources available in their communities.

The reality is that the person who is driving with dementia often has no idea that they are unsafe to drive and do not typically retire from driving without intervention from family or medical professionals.

According to the Storefront Safety Council, there are more than 100 vehicles crashing into storefronts and buildings every single day in this country. Each year in the US, as many as 16,000 people are injured and as many as 2,600 are killed in vehicle-into-building crashes. The most frequent causes are operator error (21%) and pedal error (20%).

It's important to say that just because a person is getting older does not make them an unsafe driver. Not all older drivers are unsafe behind the wheel. Some people will age gracefully and drive safely until the very end. Thankfully, most older adults will stop or restrict their own driving when they experience changes in their ability to drive because they have the insight and understanding of the risk to themselves and others. These drivers should be publicly recognized and awarded a medal for driver retirement!

The number one takeaway I share with anyone who is in a caregiving role is to try and put yourself in the shoes of the driver. Giving up the keys can be devastating news and, most, is a life-changing event. Research shows that the following six months post-driving is a critical period. Older adults who are required to stop driving are at high risk of depression and social isolation *if* alternate transportation options are not in place and support systems are lacking.

Your role and support are imperative to your loved one's driving safety. It takes courage, sensitivity, strength and love to navigate through this worrying time as you figure out if they are still safe to drive. Families, friends and support networks have an important role in helping the older driver make safe driving decisions and ensure peace of mind for the entire family. As hard it might be, spouses, adult children, or whoever may be in a caregiving role, has to take responsibility because your loved one may no longer be able to do this for themselves.

The Ride-Along: What You Can Learn from a Car Trip

As a family you will need to decide who is the best person to talk with your loved one. Often it is spouse or the adult child closest to the parent.

In my practice, I see many adult children get this wrong. Thinking the most outspoken, authoritative person is the best person to go out for a ride along and then *tell* their aging parent how it's going to be. In my experience, it's better to save this personality type for *enforcing* any driving decisions.

If you have reason to believe there may be a problem, keep in mind your aging parent may truly believe all is fine and well with their driving. They are not lying to you or trying to deceive you. Changes are occurring in certain parts of their brain. This lack of insight and awareness is not something they can control or change.

Ideally, a ride along should be planned before you have driving concerns. It will help minimize stress and anxiety for both you and your loved one if this becomes a normal part of your visit and time together. That way you can keep track and look for any changes or patterns that may be occurring.

For many families, they have not been out for a ride along with their aging parent for several years. Some family members may have the opinion their parent should stop driving but have not seen for themselves how they are driving. This isn't fair to your parent and can lead to increased anger and defensiveness from your loved one. All understandable given the situation.

If you can approach this situation from a place of love and compassion and share your worry, you will be met with less resistance. Instead of telling your loved one they have to stop driving, try saying "I'm worried about you because there are some changes going on with your health and we want to be sure you are safe, because we love you."

I am yet to meet an older driver who deliberately sets out to upset and anger their adult children. But the dynamics between a driver and their spouse/partner can be challenging. Some couples are so entrenched in negative and unhealthy relationship patterns that the driving issue adds even more fuel to the fire. If this applies to your family situation, there are experienced, skilled professionals such as geriatric care managers or family mediators who can provide necessary support. If you need a referral, please call our office at 925-249-5947.

Using a Warning Signs Checklist will give you a baseline to systematically evaluate driving performance.

And ask yourself: Would I allow my grandchild or child to ride alone with my spouse/mom/dad?

If you're unsure, then see for yourself and go for a ride along. Be familiar with the Warning Signs Checklist *before* you get in the car. Do not take the checklist with you in the car and make notes. This will only add anxiety and upset. Don't correct or criticize while in the car. Have your loved one drive to their regular destinations. If possible, drive with them several times and at different times of the day. If you are visiting from out of town or out of state, try and go out for a ride-along every day if possible.

If you are seeing some warning signs, go out for a ride-along again, the next day and observe. If you are seeing a pattern, or several warning signs, you now have firsthand experience to help start the conversation.

If your loved one is not doing well on the ride along, do not talk about this while you are in the car together. Swap driving positions if you are truly scared and get home safely. Remain calm and say as kindly as possible that after driving with them today, you are worried and think it is time for a checkup with the doctor to make sure everything is okay.

If you do not see any warning signs, then repeat the ride-along every 3-6 months or so. If there is a new health or medical condition, this time frame will need to be shortened.

The reality is we all decline in one way or another as we age. The physical and mental abilities we need to be good safe drivers may also decline.

If your loved one is refusing to allow you to ride-along and is suspicious of your motives, believing you are trying to take away the car keys, then you can always suggest an independent, objective driving assessment and "prove you wrong." Sometimes this can be a motivating factor.

Certified Driver Rehabilitation Specialists (CDRS) and Driver Rehabilitation Professionals (DRP) are qualified to conduct these types of assessments.

There are many warning signs that there may be a problem.

Warning Signs

Since driving ability seldom changes drastically in a short time, you should be able to track changes over time to get a clear picture of overall driving ability.

If you see changes in driving abilities that are happening quickly or come on suddenly, please seek medical advice and attention right away. Ensure your loved one will not continue to drive until they are seen by their physician or have a professional driving assessment.

As a caregiver, you're in the best position to observe your loved one's driving over time.

How to use this checklist:

1. Observe driving over time, keeping notes to help you understand any changes in driving ability.

2. Look for a pattern, and for any increase in warning signs. It is recommended if you see five or more warning signs, it's time to consider a cognitive driving assessment.

Driving Behaviors:

- Unaware of driving errors, belief they are still a good safe driver, lack of insight and awareness
- Declining confidence when driving
- Disorientation in familiar places
- Getting lost driving to and from the store
- Forgetting purpose of trips
- Easily distracted while driving
- Being honked at by other drivers or tells you a lot of drivers were honking when they were out driving by themselves
- Increased agitation or irritation when driving
- Uses a "co-pilot"
- Unaware of other vehicles, cyclists, or pedestrians
- Failing to use side mirrors
- Difficulty maintaining lane position
- Moves into the wrong lane
- Trouble navigating turns
- Hitting curbs
- Parking incorrectly and confusion at parking lot exits
- Riding the brake

- Confusing the brake and gas pedals
- Driving too slowly (typically) or too fast
- Incorrect signaling
- Poor judgment with left turns
- Failure to stop at stop signs or signal lights
- Stopping in traffic for no apparent reason
- Failure to notice traffic signs
- Failure to notice important activity on the side of the road
- Not anticipating potentially dangerous situations
- Delayed response to unexpected situations
- Close calls / near misses
- Ticketed moving violations or warnings
- Collision

Physical Signs

- Scrapes or dents on the car, mailbox, garage, or garden areas
- Difficulty turning head to see when backing up
- Forward head posture causing decreased neck and trunk stability
- Getting physically "stuck" during walking or other activities
- Slow motor (physical) performance
- Fatigue
- Medication side effects, e.g. daytime sleepiness, sudden fatigue, "wearing off" fluctuations
- Loss of strength or balance
- Changes in physical status
- Two or more falls in a year
- Recent surgery, hospital admission or skilled nursing rehab admission

Social Signals

- Friends or neighbors no longer want to ride with them
- Sharing that other drivers were honking when out driving

- Increased isolation or reluctance to go out
- Family members feeling unsafe as passengers

Don't ignore these signs. Use this Warning Signs Checklist and track patterns over time. It's not about one bad day—it's about consistent warning signs that raise concern.

Warning Signs Checklist QR Code

You can download a PDF that provides a warnings signs checklist using the QR code below. It includes tools for when a discussion about driving becomes necessary.

Driver Cognitive Assessment Center

If you live in the San Francisco Bay Area, our service, the Driver Cognitive Assessment Center, LLC (DCAC) provides an independent, objective cognitive driving assessment to provide fair and accurate information about driver cognitive risk and safety.

Our two-part assessment process consists of an in-office assessment and a specialized functional on-road evaluation. Together, the test results detail cognitive risk as it relates to driving, providing a baseline and peace of mind.

At DCAC, we utilize world-leading impairment assessment technology, based on science and decades of research with extensive peer review.

Drivers, their family, or any person in a caregiving role may contact our service directly. No physician referral is required. Our services are private pay.

This technology is available in other states but usually through a hospital outpatient setting. Typically, a physician referral is required.

Please contact our office if you need assistance with locating a provider using the same technology. We are more than happy to help you.

Please contact our office if you would like more information at (925)249-5947 or info@dcacbayarea.com.

We strive to be a resource for you, regardless of where your loved one lives. Please contact our office if you would like help locating a local driving assessment professional or need other resources relating to driving and transportation.

What Changes with Normal Aging

Our senses naturally change as we age, including vision, hearing, touch, taste, and smell.

Vision is especially critical for safe driving. We process visual information through our eyes, which is then interpreted by the brain, allowing us to respond with appropriate movements. When driving, this visual processing must happen quickly and accurately. In fact, it's estimated that over 90% of the information we rely on while driving comes through our eyes.

As we age, our brain's processing speed slows down. Older adults may need not only more time, but also more visual information, to decide how to respond to what's happening on the road.

By age 60, pupils can shrink to about one-third the size they were at age 20. This impacts how much light enters the eye. Many older drivers have trouble seeing at night and may struggle to recover from headlight glare—especially from newer vehicles with halogen or LED lights. Some report blurry or impaired vision when facing bright headlights. Glare recovery, or the ability to adjust after being exposed to bright light, becomes slower with age.

Night vision also declines due to reduced light reaching the retina. As a result, many older adults choose to stop driving at night altogether.

Another important factor is *perceptual reaction time*—the ability to quickly see and respond to visual cues. As we age, it often takes longer for our eyes to adjust to changes in lighting conditions. For example, moving from a dark garage into bright sunlight, or from a shaded, tree-lined street into a sunny area, can cause a delay in visual adjustment.

Light-to-dark adaptation can also be affected. Think about the experience of driving into a tunnel or underpass. It typically takes 20–30 minutes for the eyes to fully adjust to darkness, although most tunnels now include lighting to ease this transition.

We also rely on *contrast sensitivity* when driving. This is the ability to distinguish similarly colored objects—like a green car next to a row of green hedges, a gray car on a foggy day, or an orange car driving into the setting sun. Contrast sensitivity often diminishes with age, making it harder to detect these visual differences.

Peripheral vision is another key aspect of safe driving that can decline over time. Peripheral vision allows us to see motorcycles, cyclists, pedestrians, and other vehicles approaching from the side—even if they're not directly in front of us. It's also important when checking blind spots and staying aware of what's happening around the vehicle.

Dynamic visual acuity—the ability to see and interpret moving objects—is essential for driving. We rely on this skill to process the movement of cars, bikes, pedestrians, and animals on or near the road.

As we get older, many people have trouble focusing on small prints or objects. Reading a menu in a dimly lit restaurant may become challenging, and it's common to carry multiple pairs of reading glasses. This reduced ability to switch focus from near to far also affects driving, for example, when shifting your gaze from the dashboard to the road ahead to monitor traffic.

Depth perception is another visual skill that can decline with age. We need accurate depth perception to judge the distance between our vehicle and pedestrians, parked cars, and other objects nearby.

Some individuals develop floaters—small specks or strands in their field of vision—which can be distracting when driving.

A comprehensive yearly vision exam is essential for all older adults to rule out common eye conditions such as cataracts, macular degeneration, and glaucoma, all of which can impair driving ability.

Other Sensory and Physical Changes

Hearing can also change with age, particularly the ability to detect high-frequency sounds. This may make it difficult for some older drivers to hear emergency vehicles approaching.

Arthritis is common among aging adults and can affect a driver's ability to steer, operate vehicle controls, or turn their head comfortably. Back and neck pain may make it difficult to check blind spots or turn fully when changing lanes or making right turns—especially in states like California, where looking over your shoulder is a required part of the DMV Road Test. If an older adult is driving a vehicle without blind spot technology, stick-on blind spot mirrors and a larger rearview mirror can help compensate.

Some individuals experience reduced tactile sensitivity or *neuropathy* in their hands or feet, which can impair their ability to feel or respond to the pedals or steering wheel. A Certified Driving Rehabilitation Specialist (CDRS) or Driver Rehabilitation Professional (DRP) can assess these challenges and recommend adaptive equipment, such as hand or foot controls, to enhance driving safety.

Vision and Cognitive Changes

For the person living with dementia, the changes in vision, especially depth perception and useful field of view (UFOV) are magnified. The most common collision a driver with dementia will cause is turning left in front of oncoming traffic. This is because they lose depth perception early in the dementia process, which causes them to lose the ability to see how far away (or close) the vehicles are, or how fast they are approaching.

What is useful field of view? It is the area that you see and cognitively process so you can interpret which reactions you need to take when driving.

Vision & Dementia - Useful Field of View (UFOV)

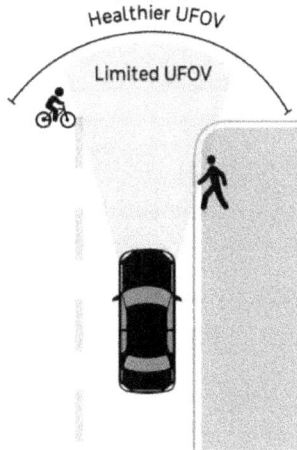

A driver with a normal useful field of view will be able to see and process the entire scene. This means they will see the cyclist and pedestrian and will plan on stopping to allow the cyclist and pedestrian to cross the street.

A driver with cognitive impairment and impaired useful field of view will only see the shaded area (limited UFOV), are unable to see and plan for the cyclist and pedestrian crossing in front and are likely to cause a collision because they are unable to plan ahead.

It's important to note that useful field of view is only one aspect of driving.

Protecting Your Loved One When They Won't Listen

There will be times when families must navigate the very difficult situation of an aging parent or loved who refuses to cooperate and is in complete denial that there are any concerns about their driving.

Fortunately, there are several options to help protect your loved one. Some families choose to hide the car keys, disconnect the battery, move the vehicle off the property, or even file down the car key. While these actions may provide an immediate—though sometimes temporary—solution, they can also lead to intense anger, resentment, or even long-term damage to the relationship between parent and adult child. Trust can quickly erode if a loved one feels deceived or excluded.

If your loved one resists going to the doctor or refuses a driving assessment, you still have options. You can—and should—write a letter to their physician. Be as clear and specific as possible in describing what you've observed and sharing your safety concerns. Physicians are often in a unique position to help initiate the conversation or provide a medical recommendation.

The timing of these conversations matters. Key moments include after a ride-along, fall, illness, hospitalization, a visit to urgent care, or a new diagnosis. Starting a new medication, or any event that could affect alertness or judgment, may also be a good opportunity to bring up driving concerns.

In many cases, there isn't one dramatic event that prompts a conversation. Instead, you may notice a gradual decline in physical strength, balance, attention, memory, or the ability to care for oneself. While some older adults will recognize these changes and reduce their driving voluntarily, others may need guidance from family to recognize when it's time to limit or stop driving.

Driving limitations can take many forms - no longer driving at night or during peak traffic hours, sticking to local routes, avoiding freeways, or not driving in unfamiliar areas or bad weather. These adjustments can help reduce risk and may allow for a more gradual transition.

Family conversations truly make a difference. What you say or don't say can influence your loved one's choices and can mean the difference between staying safe and being at risk. Although these conversations may be uncomfortable, they can support your loved one in making decisions that protect their safety and the safety of others.

Be prepared to have multiple conversations. Staying calm and respectful helps to diffuse negative emotions. Family members may have different emotional responses, some may feel angry or frustrated, others may feel guilty. Some may even deny that there's a problem. In these situations, it's important for adult children to present a united front. If your family dynamics are complex, consider involving a geriatric care manager or aging life care professional skilled in mediation and conflict resolution.

You're more likely to reach a positive outcome if your loved one is involved in the conversation, rather than simply being told what will happen. Consider the personalities involved and past experiences within your family. Some families delegate the most assertive person to lead the conversation but sometimes that person is better suited to enforcing a decision once it's made, rather than initiating the discussion.

It's important that everyone involved works together to create agreements around limiting driving. Recognizing that changes are happening can be difficult, but proactive observation and ongoing conversations can help ensure safety as time goes on.

When a driving conversation is necessary, be prepared, be strategic, and start the dialogue.

Starting the Driving Conversation

When it's time to talk about driving, it's important to be prepared, strategic, and gentle - but clear in your approach. These conversations may not be easy, but they are necessary.

Be Prepared

- Make a list of your safety and medical concerns.
- Review state licensing requirements and legal considerations.
- Plan ahead, especially if your loved one's condition is progressive or if health and finances are changing.
- Begin researching transportation alternatives and local resources. Know the alternatives BEFORE you talk about driving concerns.

Be Strategic

- Consider family dynamics. Some family members may not agree that there's a problem.
- Decide before you talk who is best suited to raise the topic in a calm, constructive way.
- Understand that your loved one may lack insight into their driving challenges.
- Expect resistance and try to understand what driving represents to them - freedom, identity, and control.
- Be sensitive but confident. You're doing this because you care.

Open the Discussion

- When appropriate, begin by acknowledging your loved one's years of safe and responsible driving.
- Gently note that things have changed.
- Be specific about what you observed.
- Speak from love and concern. Use "I" statements: "I was scared when we drove today. I'm worried about your safety."
- Invite their input. Ask how they feel about driving lately. Listen. Don't interrupt.
- Listen to their concerns and respond with empathy.

- Focus the conversation on medical conditions or cognitive changes are impacting driving abilities—don't make it personal.
- Focus on safety, not blame. Emphasize your concern for them and others.
- Talk about the real consequences of a potential crash, for themselves and others.
- Talk about liability and legal concerns.
- Highlight the value of a professional driving assessment.
- Explore alternative transportation options together.
- If needed, bring in a geriatric care manager, aging life care professional, or family mediator to help navigate conflict or tension.

In Conclusion

Talking with an aging driver about their driving can be one of the hardest conversations you will ever have. These discussions are often emotionally charged and can strain even the closest relationships. But prioritizing your loved one's safety, and the safety of everyone on the road, is what matters most.

Having "the talk" takes courage, compassion, and persistence. It's about balancing respect for their independence with a firm commitment to protecting their well-being. This isn't a one-time conversation; it's an ongoing process that requires observation, honesty, and teamwork.

Your aging parents or spouse are lucky to have you in their corner. It may feel thankless at times, but your efforts truly matter. You are making a difference—not just for them, but for everyone they share the road with. Hang in there. They need you now more than ever.

Pillar 5:
Social Interaction

[13]
Finding Strength from Afar

By
Fritzi Gros-Daillon

Caring from a distance can feel like you're living in two worlds—balancing your daily responsibilities while carrying the emotional weight of providing loving care for someone from afar. It's not always easy. The physical miles may be measurable (across the country or just across town), but the emotional distance can shift by the hour. Your caregiving tasks are part of your daily life, whether you are caregiving for an independent family member who may have physical challenges through the spectrum to those with cognitive impairment. Even in the most difficult circumstances, though, there are always strengths to uncover—places of resilience in both your loved one's situation and your own caregiving journey.

This chapter invites you to pause and reflect—not on what's missing or out of reach, but on what's already working. What systems or people are already helping? What small routines bring your loved one comfort? How are you, despite the distance, showing up in ways that matter? These moments of clarity can be grounding and deeply affirming.

As an aging-in-place specialist who has weathered the long-distance caregiving path with both parents, I offer these reflections from the trenches—where practicality meets heart, and where a sense of humor is sometimes the only thing standing between you and a good cry. I've made the panicked late-night calls, coordinated care from across the country, and learned (sometimes the hard way) what works and what doesn't. This chapter isn't about being the perfect caregiver. It's about recognizing your impact—even when you're not in the room—and building on the strengths that are already there.

Let's begin with a little grace, a dose of perspective, and the reassurance that caregiving doesn't have to be all or nothing. You're doing more than you realize—and you're not alone.

What's Working Well?

In the whirlwind of appointments, to-do lists, and late-night worries, it's easy to become laser-focused on what's going wrong. But sometimes, the best place to start is by noticing what's going right.

Maybe your mom still gets up and makes her morning tea—sure, she might leave the spoon in the sugar bowl and forget the kettle's on, but the ritual is still there. Maybe your dad still hums along to Sinatra while he eats dinner. These may seem like small things, but they're not. They're anchors. Little signs of independence, familiarity, and identity. And they matter.

Recognizing these bright spots helps shift our mindset from crisis mode to care mode—from constantly reacting to thoughtfully responding. These moments reminds you that the person you support is still here with you in meaningful ways. Your involvement—yes, even from hundreds or thousands of miles away—is part of what makes that possible.

So let's take a breath and acknowledge what's working. These wins are worth noticing, celebrating, and strengthening.

Let's look at the list below to identify the positive aspects of your loved one's current care situation. You may be surprised to see how many things are actually holding steady.

- My loved one has some consistent daily routines (e.g., meals, sleep, personal care).
- Medications are being taken as prescribed, with or without reminders.
- The home environment feels relatively safe and familiar.
- There's some level of regular social contact—neighbors, friends, faith groups, or family check-ins.
- Emergency plans are in place or are actively being developed.
- I've established communication with someone nearby—a friend, neighbor, or professional I trust.
- My loved one seems to have moments of joy, comfort, or purpose throughout the day.

What are some of the other strengths that you can see? Let's begin to document these in a journal, notebook, or even in the notes app on your smartphone. It gives us a foundation of appreciation for where we all are on the journey.

You're not just keeping track of tasks. You're supporting a life. And that's no small thing.

Recognizing Your Loved One's Abilities

Dementia has a way of gradually rearranging the mental shelves—altering things like short-term memory, planning, or complex conversations and tucking them out of reach. But if you look closely, you'll find that not everything disappears. Many beautiful abilities linger—quietly, sometimes subtly, like little treasures left on the bottom shelf.

Maybe your dad still takes pride in setting the table, even if the forks end up on the wrong side. Maybe your mom folds towels with practiced ease or lights up when she hears a familiar song from her youth. These aren't just "nice moments." They're meaningful ones. They offer comfort, dignity, and connection—not only for your loved one but for you, too.

When we focus on what remains instead of what's been lost, we open up opportunities to engage without frustration or unrealistic expectations. Supporting these remaining abilities is one of the most powerful ways to maintain your loved one's sense of self—and your relationship with them.

Here are some abilities to look for and lovingly nurture. Even small sparks can light the way.

• My loved one can still complete some daily tasks (e.g., dressing, folding laundry, light chores) with or without support.
• They respond positively to familiar activities (e.g., listening to music, spending time in nature, petting a dog or cat).
• They can express preferences and emotions—even if it's through gestures, facial expressions, or tone rather than words.
• They show pride or satisfaction after completing an activity or being included in a task.
• They enjoy touch, rhythm, routine, or sensory cues that bring comfort or calm.

Here we go with another set of journal entries! What are these abilities that we can encourage and find new ways to incorporate into daily routines?

These moments—however fleeting—are still meaningful. They are chances to preserve connection, identity, and joy. Meeting your loved one where they *are*, rather than where they *used to be*, is an act of love. And it makes a bigger difference than you might ever know.

Local and Professional Support

No caregiver is an island—especially not when you're navigating care from across the country. The truth is that long-distance caregiving only works when there's a reliable team on the ground. And that team might look a little different for every family. Maybe it's a neighbor who pops in to take the trash bins out or a home health aide who texts quick updates. Maybe it's your sister who lives twenty minutes away or a nurse at the local clinic who knows your parent by name.

These people are more than just helpers—they're lifelines. They offer eyes, ears, and hands where yours can't always be available. When you have someone nearby who cares, it's not just a logistical relief—it's emotional reassurance. It's knowing someone would notice if something seemed off. It's knowing you're not in this alone.

So, lean into those relationships. Say thank you, often and sincerely. Be clear when you need something specific, and trust that asking for help doesn't make you a burden—it makes you a strategist. A long-distance caregiver isn't "less than." You're simply operating from a different set of tools. And one of the most powerful tools in your kit is the local support you cultivate.

Take a moment to consider the people already in place, and where you might have room to build.

• Family members or friends who live nearby and check in regularly
• A trusted neighbor, church member, or community volunteer
• Hired caregivers, companions, or in-home aides
• Medical professionals who see your loved one regularly and are responsive to concerns
• Social workers, case managers, or care coordinators through insurance or local aging services
• Delivery services or tech tools (like medication reminders or camera doorbells) that fill the gaps

There are many resources available in groups and organizations such as the National Aging in Place Council with chapters throughout the U.S. Their vetted members represent a myriad of professions to support you, as the caregiver, and your family members. There are many other organizations with trained, vetted professionals to answer questions and provide hands-on solutions on home safety, health care, financial advice and more. Please check the appendix for a listing of additional resources in different categories of support services.

Practical Tools and Resources Already in Place

When you're caregiving from a distance, it can feel like you're constantly playing catch-up—juggling doctor's appointments, missed phone calls, and sudden crises. But take a moment to zoom out, and you might realize that you're already working with more tools than you thought.

Whether it's the simple brilliance of grab bars in the bathroom, a door alarm that quietly prevents a middle-of-the-night wander, or a talking clock that reminds Mom when it's time for her meds, these practical supports aren't just conveniences—they're part of your caregiving team. And sometimes, your MVP is the grocery delivery driver who shows up with fresh milk and a friendly hello.

Technology and services, when chosen wisely, can do more than just fill gaps—they can provide peace of mind, build routine, and even create moments of independence for your loved one. When you know what's already working, it's easier to identify where the true needs are—and to avoid reinventing the wheel every time something new comes up.

Let's take stock of what's already in place. You may be pleasantly surprised by how many puzzle pieces are already fitting together.

• Home safety modifications (e.g., grab bars, non-slip mats, smart sensors, motion lighting)
• Medication management systems (pill organizers, automatic dispensers, reminder apps)
• Grocery or pharmacy delivery services (scheduled or on-demand)

- Transportation support (ride services, shuttle programs, volunteer drivers)
- Communication tools (video calls, tablets, phone trees, scheduled check-ins)
- Emergency systems (medical alert devices, monitored smoke detectors, key lockboxes)
- Financial or bill management tools (auto-pay, account monitoring, trusted financial POA)

Just as you took stock of the support system earlier, now make a record of the services that you already have in place and review this list above again. What else needs to be in place, or at least be investigated, to put into place later. Not having to rush for those resources will give you time to implement more quickly with less stress and allocate efforts to meet changing circumstances.

Your Strengths as a Long-Distance Caregiver

Let's go ahead and bust a persistent myth: *You don't have to be in the same ZIP code—or even the same time zone—to be a committed, loving, and effective caregiver.*

Just because you're not physically present every day doesn't mean your role is any less valuable. In fact, long-distance caregiving requires a special kind of strength: the kind that juggles logistics, emotions, and uncertainty— often without the benefit of seeing your loved one's face at the end of the day.

If you're the one coordinating doctor's appointments from across the state, hiring in-home help, organizing medications, navigating insurance paperwork, checking in on mood and memory changes, and still remembering to send a birthday card or favorite treat—you are absolutely caregiving. And doing it with heart.

This kind of caregiving may not always be visible, but it's deeply felt. It takes mental agility, emotional endurance, and a lot of invisible labor. So take a moment—not just to recognize your responsibilities, but to acknowledge your contributions. Because you're showing up in meaningful ways, and that deserves credit.

Here are just a few of the ways long-distance caregivers support their loved ones:

- I coordinate medical appointments, home services, or support staff.
- I manage finances, insurance issues, legal paperwork, or mail.
- I stay in touch with healthcare providers, caregivers, or neighbors to stay informed.
- I offer emotional support and encouragement through phone calls, video chats, emails, or letters.
- I help with decision-making during crises or transitions.
- I advocate for my loved one's needs in healthcare, housing, or legal matters.
- I show up for birthdays, holidays, or just-because moments—however I can.

There are a myriad of ways that we, as long-distance caregivers, work for the well-being of our loved ones. The list for many caregivers is twice, three times or more the length of this list.

There's no one way to be a good caregiver. But if you're showing up with love, persistence, and problem-solving from wherever you are—you're already doing it. Don't underestimate the difference you're making. You're not "less involved." You're involved differently. And it matters more than you know.

Insights from Others

One of the unexpected blessings of long-distance caregiving is the wisdom that can come from the people who are there—on the ground, in the everyday moments you might miss. It might be the home aide who casually mentions, "Your dad lights up when the birds come to the feeder in the morning," or the neighbor who says, "Your mom always compliments my scarf when I stop by." These aren't just small observations—they're little windows into your loved one's daily life. And they matter more than you might think.

When you can't be there every day, these glimpses fill in the picture. They help you see your loved one's world not just in terms of needs and tasks, but in moments of beauty, routine, and personality. They remind you that even amid cognitive changes or physical limitations, your parent or loved one is still very much themselves in ways that matters deeply.

So don't be shy about asking. People are often happy to share what they notice—they just don't always realize how meaningful it is until you ask. A well-timed question can bring back a piece of your loved one that you thought you were losing. And those moments can be deeply grounding for everyone involved.

Here are some great prompts to help invite these insights:

• "What seems to be going well lately?"
• "What do you see them enjoying or responding to?"
• "What makes things easier or smoother during the day?"
• "Is there anything they've said or done lately that surprised or delighted you?"
• "What's one thing you think I'd love to know about how they've been doing?"

Break out the journal or notebook again and record these moments or use the notes app and dictate into your smartphone or whatever works best.

These shared observations are more than just updates—they're gifts. They help stitch together the emotional distance, and they remind you that love and connection can stretch far beyond geography. So keep asking, keep listening, and keep collecting these moments like postcards from home.

Final Thought

Let's be clear: recognizing strengths doesn't mean pretending everything is fine. It doesn't gloss over the hard days, the guilt, the worry, or the constant second-guessing. What it *does* do is bring some much-needed balance to your caregiving journey. Because when you take time to notice what's working—what's steady, what's beautiful, what's improving—you make space for hope. You honor your loved one's dignity. And you affirm your own quiet strength.

Caregiving from a distance is an emotional tightrope. You're walking between love and logistics, between showing up and letting go. It's not easy. But here's the truth: you're doing it. And not just doing it—you're doing it with heart, with creativity, with flexibility, and with more grace than you probably give yourself credit for.

Every phone call, every appointment scheduled, every thoughtful question or gentle reminder—it adds up. You may not always see the impact up close, but it's there. You are part of what's keeping things together, even across the miles.

Please hold these thoughts:

• You are a caregiver.
• You are making a difference.
• And you are doing more than you think.

Every strength, no matter how small, counts. Especially when it's built on love.

[14]

Balancing Personal and Professional Responsibilities: Senior Life Management Across America

By
Gina Knight, Dr. Lydia Manning

Introduction

> *"There are only four kinds of people in the world: those who have been caregivers, those who are currently caregivers, those who will be caregivers, and those who need caregivers."*
> – Rosalynn Carter 1987

We are a nation of caregivers navigating the complexities of supporting spouses, parents, and loved ones—and increasingly talking about the real challenges and rewards of that responsibility.

People are grappling with the logistics of caregiving, and this is becoming central to our families, our communities, our economy, and quality of life. As Gerontologists and Certified Age-In-Place Specialists, the best analogy to describe our current landscape is that families are finding themselves dealing with a complex puzzle when caring for aging loved ones. They are trying to piece together fragmented resources, information, and support without a clear picture of what the final solution should look like.

Earlier this year, Dr. Manning and I were waiting in line at a Starbucks. We happened to see three women approximately in their late 40s in what appeared to be a stressful intense conversation at a corner table. Sometimes conversational drama can be nothing new at Starbucks, so we didn't pay much attention. As we finished paying one of the ladies recognized me from being on WGN, one of our local Chicago news stations. She came over asking if I would mind joining the conversation about the challenges with her mother who was having more falling accidents within her home. I smiled saying she was in luck as I introduced Dr. Manning as we both are well qualified to provide some immediate direction.

Meet our new family client Cindy and her mother Elaine. Cindy lives with her husband and three children ages 13, 16, and 21 while working as a professor at a local university. Her mother Elaine has been living by herself in the same family home for nearly 40 years. Elaine's husband passed away in 2019. Over the past year, Elaine's health has declined, falling with greater frequency throughout the home. As we so often experience, Cindy appeared completely overwhelmed with the situation affecting both her family and professional life as a college professor of nearly 20 years. Following just our initial conversation at that corner table in Starbucks you could see the relief on Cindy's face as she found trusted partners creating a dedicated "Senior Life Management Program" for her mother Elaine. Just this initial engagement created a more productive workplace for Cindy along with an improvement in mental health for her entire family.

As Gerontologists and Certified Aging-In-Place Specialists, we are privileged to contribute our insights, drawn from extensive experience working with families who balance the challenges of caregiving with their careers.

Over the next three months Elaine's "Senior Life Management Plan" was put in place:

- Certified Senior Advisor finding the best senior living community
- Aging in Place Assessment designed to keep Elaine safe in her home until the transition
- Downsizing Plan-Prepare for packing and moving
- Assisted Living Right-size Plan for Elaine's new home
- Packing/Moving/Transitioning
- Preparing home for sale

The productivity of Cindy's workplace would have continued to decline along with additional mounting stress on her family without the support from professionals and her understanding workplace. This chapter explores the critical demand for "Employee Benefit Services" directly helping family caregivers like Cindy balance professional employment and "Senior Life Management" responsibilities. Additionally, this chapter addresses the increasing demand for Employee Benefit Services (EBS) to support the growing population of family caregivers who are navigating the dual responsibilities of professional employment and caregiving for aging loved ones.

We are committed to educating others on the essential tools and disciplines that support working family caregivers. This includes an emphasis on gerontology, the scientific study of aging, which provides a foundational understanding of the physical, emotional, and social changes older adults experience—knowledge that helps families plan proactively and compassionately. Our professional teams focus on the value of Certified Aging-in-Place services, which involve assessments and home modifications that allow older adults to live safely and independently in their own homes for as long as possible. This can significantly reduce stress for working caregivers who are trying to coordinate safe living environments for loved ones while maintaining their professional and family responsibilities.

Concierge Senior Transitioning refers to the comprehensive support offered during major life changes such as downsizing, relocating to a senior living community, or preparing a home for sale. These services relieve caregivers of time-consuming, emotionally taxing responsibilities that often conflict with work schedules. In addition, we emphasize access to mental health resources and community-based support, which are vital for caregiver resilience. From counseling and peer groups to respite care and adult day programs, these resources help caregivers manage stress, avoid burnout, and stay engaged in both their caregiving and professional roles. We are honored to contribute, drawing from our experiences from our nation of family caregivers.

Part 1: Our American Demographic Reality

The United States is an aging nation, with a staggering reality of 10,000 people turning 65 and now 75 years old each day. Important statistics to note:

1. For the first time ever in 2030, the United States will have a greater population over the age of 65 than under the age of 18.

2. By 2050, 1 in 5 Americans will be over the age of 65 with 15-18 million over the age of 85 and the fastest-growing segment of our population.

3. The family caregiving role is increasingly the norm with over 50 million family members in the U.S. providing care for a loved one each year.

The American Family Caregiver
"As you grow older, you will discover that you have two hands — one for helping yourself, the other for helping others."
– Audrey Hepburn

Make no mistake, you will become a caregiver in some capacity during your lifetime. This includes caregiving responsibilities for a loved one, neighbor, friend or even yourself. How long, when, where and at what capacity is based on so many life conditions. Simultaneously, taking place with the critical responsibilities of family caregiving is the necessity of working for a lengthier timeframe later in life. Most Americans enter the workforce around age 20 working at least part-time well into their 70s. Working family caregivers is the economic reality of our society. All employees and owners are impacted regardless of their profession along with their clientele and the people they serve.

As of 2025, there are an estimated 70 million Americans aged 65 and older, underscoring the urgency of addressing the challenges faced by our families, our communities, our economy and quality of life. As a result, identifying trusted resources for proper planning is the beginning of the multitude of challenges facing family caregivers. From scheduling doctor visits, arranging transportation, finding better living arrangements, transitioning to a senior living community or dealing with home modifications, family caregivers face a myriad of challenges. Many patient advocacy organizations have (90%) of their respondents reporting spending a minimum of 10 hours per week on caregiving related tasks and (50%) indicated they spent at least 20 hours per week.

Family caregivers typically look after spouses, parents, and other relatives such as grandparents, and parents-in-law. However, this also extends to friends, neighbors and even you. We have become a nation of care storytellers talking about their spouse, parents and loved ones. Everyone is telling more care management stories with detail and how caregiving is central to our families, our communities, our economy, and quality of life.

Our biggest challenge arising from our current demographic reality is the increasing strain it places on family relationships and the ability to manage and care for a loved one at any point in your life. Where do I go for support and services specifically dedicated to older adults who can immediately make my life easier? Majority of the time, family caregivers ask themselves who, what, where, when and how do I even begin to help my aging parents, spouse or loved one. The good news is that many professionals like the contributors within this book are aware of the stress and hardship associated with caring for an aging parent, spouse or loved one.

Companies support and advocate for older adults and caregivers, such as Kastle Keeper and Circle of Life Consulting, Inc., could not properly support aging families without The National Aging in Place Council. This trusted network of professionals connects older adults, their loved ones and caregivers with local professionals who provide the support needed to deal with the challenges of aging at home or in a senior living community.

Part 2: The Intersection of Caregiving and the Workplace
Our invisible workplace reality

Challenges are felt by family caregivers and American businesses alike which collectively lose as much as $34 billion each year due to the caregiving responsibilities of both full-time and part-time workers over the age of 50. Caregiving support is not only a family issue but a business issue with a direct financial impact on all organizations regardless of size. Let's start out by saying family caregivers are disproportionately women with an average age of 46 years old in their prime working years. The reality of balancing work and family caregiving responsibilities affect more than 1 in 5 Americans and expected to double within the next 20 years. According to "World at Work" a non-profit organization supporting HR professionals since 1955 surveyed recently 55% of all employee respondents used paid time off (PTO) to manage caregiving responsibilities. Of all those working family caregivers surveyed, over 90%, nearly everyone said offering specific caregiving benefits would enhance their quality of life, leading to improved productivity at work and overall well-being.

According to AARP, to meet family caregiving responsibilities:

• 32% have shifted from full-time to part-time work
• 27% have turned down a promotion, losing out on increased family income
• 16% have stopped working, left their company or sold their business

As the need for elder care continues to rise, it's increasingly important for businesses to recognize the impact family caregiving responsibilities have on their employees and the profitability and success of their company. Fortunately, research shows that a supportive workplace with resources for family caregiving creates a loyal and motivated workforce. The result being a company with enhanced productivity, improved employee retention and greater profitability. Companies need to decide what type of senior related services to prioritize based on the understanding of their workforce.

The Face of Family Caregiving

There is no shortage of new research from SHRM (Society for Human Resource Management) spotlighting real challenges for family caregivers. What might be surprising is that what today's family caregiver looks like because it's not just the "empty nest" parents with kids out of college taking care of Mom and Dad.

• According to the U.S. Bureau of Labor Statistics, over 30% of employed people aged 18 and over provide care on any given day.

• Nearly 1 in 4 working caregivers are part of the "sandwich generation," juggling elder care and childcare.

Career Sacrifices

Forty-two percent of working caregivers say their caregiving responsibilities hinder career advancement. Nearly half (47%) would take a career shift for better caregiving support.

Resume Gap

More than half (54%) of caregivers with a gap in employment say caregiving was the reason.

What's worse, 74% of unemployed caregivers trying to return to work say that gap has negatively impacted their job prospects. Companies fail to recognize or discuss how specifically dealing with family caregiving affects employee turnover and profitability.

Exceptional Managers and Leaders

The workplace environment that delivers the support needed to working family caregivers will without question have better leaders in their organizations. Family caregivers with support services will excel better at their company in resolving conflicts with greater skills in coaching and mentorship. These characteristics are essential for a successful organization.

This is the new face of our workplace and communities and is the present and future of our economy.

Jennifer's Grandmother

The Chicagoland National Aging in Place Council had their annual member event at Gibsons Bar & Steakhouse in suburban Chicago earlier this year. Meet Jennifer, a 33-year-old hostess and event planner who helped us organize such a fantastic luncheon for over 50 professionals.

Jennifer, recently married, loves her job working full-time close to home at Gibsons. Following our event, after everyone left, she pulled me aside with tears in her eyes saying, "I can't believe what you do." In all honesty, it's one of the greatest compliments we receive as professionals making lives easier for working caregivers. Jennifer recently lost her father to cancer and her mother currently lives in another state. Jennifer has a grandmother living at home alone and struggling with early onset dementia. Grandma's condition has declined dramatically over the past six months. She has struggled most recently with falls, confusion, and anger.

With all the ongoing changes in Medicare and Medicaid, families are experiencing a much more difficult challenge to navigate the support they need for everyday activities of daily living. Jennifer could never have imagined this caregiving responsibility as she started her new marriage and career job at the restaurant. Jennifer's family caregiving responsibility has put an emotional strain on her marriage and performance at work along with her relationship with colleagues and friends.

In our 20-minute conversation we were able to provide connections to three NAIPC (National Aging in Place Council) trusted professionals best suited for Jennifer's grandmother at this time.

1. Senior Living Advisor: Locating potential memory care facilities.

2. Dementia Care Professional: Clinical psychological evaluation to determine current state of dementia.

3. Certified Aging-in-Place Specialist: Keeping Jennifer's grandmother safe in her home prior to relocating to a memory care community.

Jennifer, along with millions of working family caregivers, are amazingly resilient but they can't thrive along with their loved ones without flexibility, understanding and support, especially in the workplace where well over

50% of our time is spent during our adult lives. The future of the American workplace must be built with the family caregiver in mind because providing support and resources is directly tied to the economic success of the company and our society. The results will pay dividends to retain the best talent, fostering loyalty with a culture and community rooted in humanity.

Senior Benefit Service Programs providing family caregiving resources is almost non-existent in the corporate or public sector workplace. This is a highly specialized and necessary healthcare benefit because balancing work and family caregiving without support can be the great "productivity killer" both at home and in the workplace. Research shows that a supportive workplace with resources for family caregiving creates a loyal and motivated workforce. The result being a company with enhanced productivity, improved employee retention and greater profitability.

The demand for the family is very clear. Providing support to employees during a challenging time as they manage family responsibilities for an aging spouse, parent or loved one is vital to the success of an organization. The greatest value for family caregivers is accessibility to trusted industry experts. Professional Senior Advisors vs on-line marking platforms should be the voice of reason for the family providing a trusted place to begin.

Part 3: Finding Clarity in the Chaos

Gerontologists and Certified Aging-in-Place experts are quite often great first responders for helping family caregivers and companies looking to build a Senior Benefit Service Program for a more productive workplace.

Role of Certified Aging-in-Place Specialists and Gerontologists

Most older adults have the desire to remain in their home forever with the mantra "I don't want to go anywhere." Aging in place requires a comprehensive approach, addressing not only the physical needs of older adults but also the emotional, social, and environmental factors allowing for independent living. Trusted professionals play an essential role in implementing solutions that help older adults remain in their homes and independent living communities safe, happy and healthy. The important prerequisite of implementing an individual Aging in Place plan is vital to the success of remaining safe and independent in your home for as long as possible.

The Importance of Certified Aging-in-Place Assessments

The most important factor is to properly complement the current mobility and medical condition with the required modifications to the home. This becomes the blueprint for successful Age-in-Place living for the family and their loved ones. This enables the older adult to move forward with safe modifications most often in the bathroom, kitchen, laundry, and/or entrance way areas.

Concierge Senior Transitioning Services

Perhaps one of the biggest stressful lifetime changes for an older adult is relocating to another home or senior living community. Endless details are required of the family caregiver managing the following overwhelming area:

• Certified Senior Advisor select best senior living community
• Developing a right-size plan
• Professional Downsizing/Donating personal property
• Professional Senior Move Management
• Packing and full new home setup
• Preparing the family home for sale
• Senior Real Estate Sales Partner

Providing employees with access to a trusted concierge all-inclusive senior transition specialist is vital for both the well-being of the employee and productivity of the company where they work. Senior transition experts help manage every aspect of the relocation, helping family caregivers maintain their well-being and economic stability.

Senior Life Management for Family Caregivers

Even well-prepared families ask themselves "who, what, where, when and how do I even begin" to help manage all the moving parts in the life of parents, spouse or a loved one. The senior benefit service here is a compassionate network connecting working family caregivers to senior life management professionals. Below are the key areas that touch all our lives:

• In-Home Medical Care
• In-Home Companion Care
• Certified Home Modification Plan
• Elder Law and Estate Planning
• Finance and Insurance Specialists
• Socialization and Mental Health Services

Senior Crisis Management is a more stressful role the family caregiver may experience at some point while they are working. They are the unexpected crisis events happening in the lives of older adults. Here are some common examples:

1. Mom fell and needs to go to the hospital.

2. Mom or Dad is discharging tomorrow. How will I even get them up the eight stairs in front of their home.

3. My spouse is wandering outside of the home. I need to immediately find them a memory care community.

4. Dad can no longer take care of himself and needs to move from independent living to an assisted living arrangement.

5. My grandmother had an unexpected accident, and we need to immediately make home modifications so she can remain in her home upon return from the hospital.

Community Programs and Training Opportunities

Local community resources are essential in supporting family caregivers and helping aging individuals live independently. Senior centers, adult daycare programs, and respite care services provide caregivers with much-needed relief, ensuring their loved ones receive quality care while alleviating the pressure and responsibilities on caregivers. These services offer temporary care, socialization opportunities, and access to community resources, creating an environment where caregiving and work can coexist. Collaboration among community-based networks, local organizations, and support groups is vital to providing caregivers with the assistance they need without compromising their professional responsibilities.

Government programs such as Medicaid, Supplemental Security Income (SSI), and the National Family Caregiver Support Program also play a key role in supporting both caregivers and aging adults. These programs provide financial assistance, training, counseling services, and respite care to reduce the emotional and financial challenges caregivers face. Access to these resources allow caregivers to continue their caregiving roles while safeguarding their own well-being.

To foster a caregiving-friendly environment, businesses, policymakers, and caregivers must take proactive steps. Businesses can implement flexible work hours, expand Family and Medical Leave benefits, and create employee assistance programs (EAPs) tailored to caregiving support. Policymakers should advocate for policies that provide financial aid and improve access to community services, while caregivers should actively seek available resources to balance caregiving with self-care. Employers also play a crucial role in supporting caregivers by encouraging self-care practices, ensuring that caregivers remain healthy, engaged, and productive.

Building a strong support system is key to preventing burnout and sustaining caregiver well-being. Caregiving should never be a solo effort - it requires a team that includes family, friends, and professional partners. Employers can play a proactive role by offering caregiver support groups, providing training on eldercare issues, and linking employees with community-based services. Equally important is promoting self-care for caregivers. Maintaining one's own health, emotional balance, and identity outside the caregiving role is not indulgent - it is essential. Whether it's through counseling, mindfulness practices, or simply carving out regular time for rest, supporting caregivers means making space for their wholeness as human beings.

Part 4: Final Thoughts

As we come across family caregivers balancing their personal lives with their professional workplace, our main goal is to reduce the stress in their lives. Senior Benefit Service Programs reducing the chaotic lives of their family caregiving employees will be well on their way to accomplishing the following:

1. More productive and profitable workplace
2. Happy and healthier employees
3. Greater communication and image within their community

As the demand for family caregiving grows, businesses must take an active role in supporting their caregiving employees. The intersection of caregiving and professional responsibilities presents challenges for both caregivers and organizations. Offering Employee Benefit Services (EBS) like flexible work schedules, caregiving leave, and Employee Assistance Programs (EAPs) can reduce the strain on caregivers. These initiatives not only ease stress but also improve job satisfaction, employee retention, and productivity. As the caregiving landscape evolves, it is increasingly important for businesses to implement strategies that support the caregiving role, fostering a healthier, more productive workforce.

Integrating caregiving support into workplace policies is crucial for the future of family caregiving. A collaborative approach involving businesses, policymakers, and caregivers is needed to create supportive environments. Expanding access to community resources, financial assistance, and work-life balance will help build a sustainable caregiving model that benefits both caregivers and aging individuals. These initiatives will not only support individual families but also contribute to a more resilient society as we navigate the challenges of an aging population.

What Should You Do Next?

Congratulations on reaching the end of this book. By taking the time to read, reflect, and learn, you've already taken an important step in supporting your loved one - and yourself. Caregiving, whether near or from a distance, is a journey filled with both challenges and rewards. The knowledge, insights, and resources shared in these pages are here to guide you, but the next step is action.

Start by revisiting the sections that resonated most with you. The contents page summaries are designed to help you quickly identify the topics that meet your immediate needs. Perhaps it's learning practical ways to support a loved one with cognitive changes, building a local support network, or integrating technology into daily care. Whatever speaks to you, take that insight and try applying it this week - even one small action can make a meaningful difference.

The authors encourage you to extend your learning beyond these pages. Visit their websites for blogs, downloadable resources, and tools designed to make caregiving easier and more effective. (See the "Biographical Index of Contributing Authors" for more information). You will find practical guidance, inspiring stories, and advice that complements what you've learned here. Additionally, the National Aging in Place Council offers a wealth of vetted resources - from professional support services to safety solutions - that can strengthen your caregiving approach and bring peace of mind.

Reflection is a powerful tool: pause to acknowledge what you're already doing well. Celebrate your successes, even the small ones, and recognize the positive impact your care has on your loved one's life. Caregiving is not about perfection; it's about presence, consistency, and love.

Finally, remember that you are not alone. Reach out, ask for help, and use the tools, networks, and knowledge available to you. Implement what you've learned here, take note of what works, and adjust as needed. Every step you take, no matter how small, reinforces your loved one's well-being and preserves your own energy and resilience.

This book is your starting point so let it inspire action, curiosity, and confidence. Now, take a deep breath, pick one step that feels right today, and move forward. Your caregiving journey continues, stronger and more informed, with hope, insight, and support by your side.

Biographical Index of Contributing Authors

Jocelyn Brown, PhD

Jocelyn Brown is a multidisciplinary scholar with a Ph.D. in Gerontology and master's degrees in Sociology and Psychology, currently serving as an Assistant Professor of African American Studies at Ohio University. Her work centers on the intersections of race, health, labor, and place, especially in the context of Black life in Appalachia.

Julie A. Brown, PhD

Julie Brown is an Associate Professor of Gerontology at Ohio University specializing in AgeTech and Aging in Place. Her research explores technology use, age-inclusive design, and the lived experiences of older adults and caregivers. With a focus on applied innovation, Dr. Brown partners across sectors to reimagine aging through equitable, human-centered solutions that bridge research, caregiving, and everyday life.

Dr. DeLon Canterbury

Dr. DeLon Canterbury, PharmD, BCGP, is the founder and president of GeriatRx, a pharmacist-led clinical practice dedicated to safe medication use and deprescribing for older adults. A nationally recognized speaker, consultant, and advocate for aging in place, Dr. Canterbury partners with families, healthcare systems, and organizations like the National Aging in Place Council to improve quality of life through thoughtful medication management. Learn more at www.geriatricrx.com.

Mark Conacher

Mark Conacher is an award-winning leader and Managing Director of SENSTEC USA. With over 30 years in the Kitchen & Bathroom Industry, he serves as an Executive Advisor to the British Institute of Fitted Interiors Specialists (BIFIS) in the UK and was named a Praiseworthy Pick for NKBA's Kitchen & Bath Magazine Person of the Year in the US. Based in Vancouver, Canada, Mark champions higher installation standards and safer bathroom design to deliver practical solutions that support slip safety in the shower. You can visit his website at: www.senstec-usa.com.

Israel Cross, PhD, ECHM, CAPS

Dr. Israel Cross is a public health gerontologist and U.S. Public Health Service Commissioned Corps officer with more than 15 years of experience addressing the complex, multigenerational challenges of aging across the life course. With expertise in healthcare delivery, quality assurance and performance improvement (QAPI), and community engagement, he is committed to expanding access to high-quality care for older adults and caregivers. His contributions to national patient safety span diverse care settings—including Federally Qualified Health Centers, nursing homes, home health agencies, hospitals, and end-stage renal disease facilities—where he has helped shape and implement meaningful quality improvement initiatives. As President of the National Aging in Place Council, Dr. Cross champions the dignity, autonomy, and well-being of aging individuals, advancing preventive strategies and system-level solutions that strengthen support across generations. A Certified Aging-in-Place Specialist and Dementia Practitioner, he leverages program evaluation, strategic partnerships, and stakeholder engagement to drive transformative efforts in public health and aging. Learn more about Dr. Cross at LinkedIn: www.linkedin.com/in/israel-cross-phd.

James Donnelly

James Donnelly founded and leads Safe Haven Insurance Agency, where he empowers individuals and families with smart Medicare, insurance, and retirement planning rooted in real-life lessons. Raised in a blue-collar, small-business family, he saw firsthand the consequences of inadequate financial protection. He's committed to helping people break the cycle by protecting today, planning for tomorrow. For more information, visit www.safehaveninsuranceagency.com.

Sean Fitzgerald
Sean Fitzgerald is the President of TruBlue Home Service Ally (www.trublueally.com), a franchise system dedicated to aging in place through home repair, safety modifications, and subscription-based maintenance programs. With more than 25 years of franchising experience and a strong focus on the senior care industry, Sean has successfully led the growth of multiple national organizations. Inspired by his own family's experience caring for aging parents and in-laws, he leads TruBlue's commitment to helping older adults live safely, independently, and comfortably at home - while bringing peace of mind to their loved ones.

Fritzi Gros-Daillon
Fritzi Gros-Daillon is NAIPC 2024 Member of the Year, has been a CAPS Instructor since 2015 and 2019 NAHB Educator of the Year. With Household Guardians, she offers home safety consulting. She is Director of Education for Age Safe America. She has served on the boards for NARI San Diego and SD County Council on Aging. She conducts AARP Home Fit training. She is a national speaker, podcast and TV guest on aging in place. She authored award-winning "Grace and Grit: Insights to Real Life Challenges of Aging". Learn more at www.householdguardians.com.

Melanie Henry
Melanie Henry is the founder and CEO of Driver Cognitive Assessment Center (DCAC), specializing in cognitive evaluations of experienced drivers. A Licensed Driving Instructor and Driver Rehabilitation Professional, she brings decades in social welfare, risk assessment, and child protection. As a volunteer driver medical-ride coordinator, she saw the

need for objective driver cognitive assessments and created DCAC. Melanie co-authored NAIPC's "Difficult Aging in Place Conversations," speaks on aging and driving across the Bay Area, volunteers with CARFIT, and launched Turn Signal Driving School. Learn more at www. dcacbayarea.com.

Eve Hill
Eve Hill, Founder of Customized Aging, is a Certified Aging-in-Place Specialist (CAPS), REALTOR®, and outspoken advocate for accessible design and ageism awareness. She project-manages the Aging in Place process for older adults and their families and partners with senior sector professionals to spark proactive planning around the longevity lifestyle. Eve's previous work in nonprofits and TV writing informs her educational outreach and creative communications style. Learn more at www. customizedaging.com.

Gina Knight
Gina Knight is a Certified Aging-in-Place Specialist, Founder & Chairman, National Aging in Place Council – Chicagoland; Board of Directors for the National Aging in Place Council in Washington DC. and Real Estate Broker for 25 + years. Ms. Knight is the President of Kastle Keeper in Oak Brook, Illinois and Senior Concierge Professionals in Naples, Florida. As a highly regarded professional, Gina has earned the trust and confidence of her partners with a reputation of always working in the best interests of the senior and their family. Learn more at www.kastlekeeperllc.com. www. scpnaples.com.

Mary Lynch
Mary Lynch blends nearly 30 years of real estate expertise with a heartfelt mission inspired by caring for her grandfather. As Founder and Chair of the Greater Baltimore Chapter of the National Aging in Place Council, she is committed to building community resources that empower older adults and their families. A Certified Senior Advisor (CSA), Senior Home

Coach ™, and Seniors Real Estate Specialist (SRES), Mary helps clients navigate downsizing, accessible housing, and long-term planning with warmth, clarity, and deep personal connection. Learn more at www. movewithmarylynch.com.

Dr. Lydia Manning

Dr. Lydia Manning is a gerontologist, educator, and entrepreneur, with a rich background in aging and life course transitions. Lydia serves as CEO of Circle Life Consulting, Inc., where her dynamic leadership contributes to advancements in the field of aging. She also services as Director of Professional Education and Consulting Services at Miami University's Scripps Gerontology Center. Her work centers on translating gerontological research into practical solutions for organizations and communities. Lydia's research interests include resilience, spirituality, gerontology education, and GeronTech. Learn more at www. lydiamanning.com.

Chris Orestis

Chris Orestis, CSA President of Retirement Genius, is a nationally recognized expert in retirement, finance, and aging. He's a former D.C. lobbyist, political operative, and senior issues advocate with 25+ years of industry experience. One of the most quoted experts in the insurance and financial services industry-- he has appeared in The New York Times, Wall Street Journal, CNBC, AARP Magazine, USA Today, NBC News, Fox News, and numerous other media outlets including being a guest expert on over 100 radio programs and TV news segments.

Cindi Petito

Cindi Petito, OTR/L, ATP, CEAC, CAPS, is an occupational therapist with over 30 years of experience, currently serving as the Director of Live at Home at VGM Group, Inc. She has more than 26 years specializing in home accessibility, complex rehab technology, and assistive technologies, with a focus on aging adults and individuals with traumatic injuries and neurodegenerative diseases. Prior, Cindi owned a private therapy practice for over 20 years, providing services to Medicare and Medicaid beneficiaries. She serves on the board of RESNA and holds a position on the board of directors for NAIPC. Cindi has a B.A. in Health Science and an MBA in Healthcare Administration. Website: https://www.vgm.com/communities/live-at-home/.

Nicole Ramer

Nicole Ramer is a Certified Professional Organizer®, Certified Senior Move Manager® and Chronic Disorganization Specialist®. Since 2012, she has helped older adults and their families declutter, downsize, and transition to safer living environments. Nicole is the founder of Organized Haven, a full-service Senior Move Management® company in Lakeland, Florida, and the Executive Director of Safe Moves for Seniors Polk. She leads Downsizers Club to support families in planning future moves. You can learn more at www.organizedhaven.com.

Felicia Saraceno

Felicia Saraceno is a Senior Living Expert and REALTOR® based in Naples, Florida, with two decades in real estate and over a decade in senior living leadership. A Certified Dementia Practitioner and Senior Real Estate Specialist, she has guided hundreds of older adults and their families through downsizing, housing transitions, and aging-in-place planning. As co-founder of the Productive Aging Collective, Felicia is passionate about educating, empowering, is a national speaker and preparing aging adults in Southwest Florida and beyond to navigate life's changes and unexpected challenges with confidence and dignity. Learn more at https://linktr.ee/NaplesParadiseLiving.

Endnotes and Additional Resources

Chapter 2: Caring Through Clutter: How Caregivers Can Create a Safer, Simpler Home for Their Loved Ones

1. Centers for Disease Control and Prevention (CDC). "Falls: Data & Research." Accessed September 17, 2025. https://www.cdc.gov/falls/data-research/index.html.

2. Buysee, M. K. "Senior Move Managers® Are Dedicated to Reducing the Emotional and Physical Stress That Accompanies Transitions." *National Association of Senior & Specialty Move Managers*. Accessed September 17, 2025. https://www.nasmm.org.

Chapter 4: The Caregiver's Advantage: Ageism Awareness

Note: For consistency across this collection, all chapter endnotes are presented as lists. In this chapter, sources are listed in the order they appeared in the text to preserve the original citation sequence.

3. World Health Organization. "Ageism." Accessed September 17, 2025. https://www.who.int/health-topics/ageism.

4. Levy, Becca R., Mark D. Slade, Suzanne R. Kunkel, and Stanislav V. Kasl. "Longevity Increased by Positive Self-Perceptions of Aging." *Journal of Personality and Social Psychology* 83, no. 2 (2002): 261–70. https://pubmed.ncbi.nlm.nih.gov/12150226.

5. Graham, Carol, and J. Ruiz Pozuelo. "Happiness, Stress, and Age: How the U Curve Varies across People and Places." *Journal of Population Economics* 30, no. 1 (2017): 225–64.

6. Rauch, Jonathan. *The Happiness Curve: Why Life Gets Better after 50.* New York: St. Martin's Press, 2018.

7. Mather, Mara, and Laura L. Carstensen. "Aging and Motivated Cognition: The Positivity Effect in Attention and Memory." *Trends in Cognitive Sciences* 9, no. 10 (October 2005): 496–502. https://pubmed. ncbi.nlm.nih.gov/16154382.

8. Weiss, Alan. *Threescore and More: Applying the Assets of Maturity, Wisdom, and Experience for Personal and Professional Success.* New York: Routledge, 2018.

9. Birren, James E., and Donna Deutchman. *Guiding Autobiography Groups for Older Adults.* Baltimore: Johns Hopkins University Press, 1991.

10. Aronson, Louise. *Elderhood: Redefining Aging, Transforming Medicine, Reimagining Life.* New York: Bloomsbury Publishing, 2019.

11. Shaw, Carrie. "Beyond CAEZ: LeadingAgeVA2025—The Purpose Equation." LinkedIn post, June 2025. https://www.linkedin.com/posts/ carrieeshaw_beyoncaez-leadingageva2025-thepurposeequation-activity-7335748936533458945-GQvd.

12. Marshall, Consuela. Interview by author. *Finding a Foothold* podcast. Accessed September 17, 2025. https://www.findingafoothold.com.

13. Bisconti, Taylor, Jessica Sublett, and Amanda Chasteen. "Benevolent Ageism: Exploring Its Boundary Conditions, Generalizability, and Correlates." *Innovation in Aging* 4, Suppl. 1 (2020): 568–69. https:// academic.oup.com/innovateage/article/4/Supplement_1/568/6036238.

14. Marshall, Consuela. Interview by author.

15. Kontos, Pia, Karen L. Miller, and Gail J. Mitchell. "Relational Citizenship: Supporting Embodied Selfhood and Relationality in Dementia Care." *Sociology of Health & Illness* 39, no. 2 (2017): 182–98. https://onlinelibrary.wiley.com/doi/10.1111/1467-9566.12453.

16. Fuchs, Danniel. "Adapting Your Home to Aging in Place." Presentation, Burbank Adult Center, 2025. Author of *The Ultimate Guide to Multigenerational Living*. https://www.multi-gen.com.

17. Kitwood, Thomas. *Dementia Reconsidered: The Person Comes First.* Buckingham: Open University Press, 1997.

18. Greenhouse, Esther. "Enabling by Design: Leveraging Home Features for Physical and Financial Independence in Retirement." *Certified Senior Advisors Journal*, no. 85 (2021): 26.

19. Center for Universal Design. "Universal Design Definition." Accessed September 17, 2025. https://www.universaldesign.org/definition.

20. Gendron, Tracey. *Ageism Unmasked*. Lebanon, NH: Steerforth Press, 2022.

21. AARP. "Home and Community Preferences Survey 2024." Washington, DC: AARP, December 10, 2024. https://www.aarp.org/pri/topics/livable-communities/housing/2024-home-community-preferences.

22. Vespa, Jonathan, Jeremy Engelberg, and Wan He. "Old Housing, New Needs: Are U.S. Homes Ready for an Aging Population?" P23-217. Washington, DC: U.S. Census Bureau, May 15, 2020.

23. Rebuilding Together. "Impact Measurement Project Evaluation Report, 2020–2021." Washington, DC: Rebuilding Together, October 2021.

24. Coalition for Home Repair. "Falls Prevention Cohort Summary." Evaluation conducted with HomesRenewed Resource Center and East Tennessee State University College of Public Health, December 2023. https://coalitionforhomerepair.org.

25. Carnemolla, Phillippa, and Catherine Bridge. "Housing Design and Community Care: How Home Modifications Reduce Care Needs of Older People and People with Disability." *International Journal of Environmental Research and Public Health* 16, no. 11 (2019): 1951. https://www.mdpi.com/1660-4601/16/11/1951.

26. USC Family Caregiver Support Center. "C.A.L.M. (Caregivers Are Learning More)." Accessed September 17, 2025. https://gero.usc.edu/centers/fcsc.

27. Silverstone, Barbara, and Helen K. Hyman. *You and Your Aging Parent: A Family Guide to Emotional, Social, Health, and Financial Problems.* New York: Oxford University Press, 1989.

28. Australian Human Rights Commission. *Changing Perspectives: Testing an Ageism Intervention.* Canberra: AHRC, 2023.

Chapter 8: Aging in Motion: Staying Active with Mobility Supports?

29. Centers for Disease Control and Prevention Foundation. "Preventing Older Adult Falls and Fall Injuries." Accessed September 17, 2025. https://www.cdcfoundation.org/programs/falls.

30. Fall Prevention Foundation. "Walking Aids to Prevent Falls: A Comprehensive Guide to Safe Mobility for Seniors." Accessed September 17, 2025. https://fallpreventionfoundation.org/2025/06/26/walking-aids-to-prevent-falls-a-comprehensive-guide-to-safe-mobility-for-seniors.

The following photos are included in this book. Photo credits and sources are listed below to be used in Aging in Place Conversations: The Caregiver's Edition, 2025:

1. Canes and Crutches: "Man walking with cane," iStock by Getty Images

2. Walkers: "Couple walking in park, woman using walker," iStock by Getty Images

3. Four Wheeled Walkers: "Couple walking on sidewalk, woman using four wheeled walker," iStock by Getty Images

4. Manual Wheelchairs: "Middle age person sitting in manual wheelchair in park," iStock by Getty Images.

5. Motorized Scooters: "Senior man sitting in motorized scooter on the golf course," iStock by Getty Images.

6. Power Wheelchairs: "Senior man sitting in a power wheelchair on a sidewalk, green grass behind him," iStock by Getty Images.

7. Personal Vehicles: "Man wearing a t-shirt that says "Navy" standing behind a car equipped with a lift," Photo courtesy of Harmar Mobility, LLC, used with permission.

Chapter 12: Driver Safety: A Caregiver's Guide

31. National Safety Council and Caring.com. "Nationwide Survey of Baby Boomers, 2008."

32. American Automobile Association Foundation. "Rates of Motor Vehicle Crashes, Injuries, and Deaths in Relation to Driver Age in the United States, 2014–2015." Accessed September 17, 2025. https://aaafoundation.org/rates-motor-vehicle-crashes-injuries-deaths-relation-driver-age-united-states-2014-2015/.

33. Mishori, Ranit, MD, MHS, FAAFP. "The Older Driver." *American Family Physician* 101, no. 10 (2020): 625–29.

34. DriveABLE. "Impairica Impairment Assessment Technologies." Accessed September 17, 2025. https://impirica.tech/driveable/.

35. Alzheimer's Association. "Alzheimer's Facts and Figures." Accessed September 17, 2025. https://www.alz.org/getmedia/ef8f48f9-ad36-48ea-87f9-b74034635c1e/alzheimers-facts-and-figures.pdf.

36. Kelleher, Shannon, Maura Powell, Alexander K. Gonzalez, Shukai Cheng, Nicole Koepke, Elizabeth A. Walshe, Jamillah Millner, Joshua C. Fischer, Colleen M. Schlotter, Flaura K. Winston, and Alexander G. Fiks. "The Annals of Family Medicine." *Annals of Family Medicine* 22, no. 4 (2024): 357. https://www.annfammed.org/content/22/4/357/tab-e-letters.

37. Journal of the American Board of Family Medicine. "The Role of Physicians in Assessing Older Drivers: Barriers, Opportunities, and Strategies." 2010.

38. Storefront Safety Council. Accessed September 17, 2025. https://www.storefrontsafety.org.

Chapter 14: Balancing Personal and Professional Responsibilities: Senior Life Management across America

39. AARP. "The Financial Impact of Caregiving on the U.S. Workforce." Accessed September 17, 2025. https://www.aarp.org/workforce.

40. Family Caregiver Alliance. "Caregiver Statistics: Demographics." Accessed September 17, 2025. https://www.caregiver.org/caregiver-statistics-demographics.

41. Gallup-Healthways. "Gallup-Healthways Well-Being Index." 2011.

42. Joseph, L. M. "Aging in Place: Interprofessional Approaches to Empower Informal Caregivers." *The Journal for Nurse Practitioners* 19, no. 1 (2023): 104412. https://doi.org/10.1016/j.nurpra.2022.07.020.

43. MetLife Mature Market Group, National Alliance for Caregiving, and the University of Pittsburgh Institute on Aging. *The MetLife Study of Working Caregivers and Employer Health Costs: Double Jeopardy for Baby Boomers Caring for Their Parents.* 2010.

44. National Alliance for Caregiving and AARP. *Caregiving in the U.S. 2020.* Washington, DC: NAC and AARP, 2021. https://www.caregiving.org/caregiving-in-the-us-2020/.

45. Northwestern National Life Insurance Company. *The Impact of Caregiving on Employee Productivity and Absenteeism.* 1999.

46. Society for Human Resource Management (SHRM). "Workplace Eldercare Benefits and Their Impact on Employees." SHRM Press Release, December 2003. https://www.shrm.org.

47. University of Texas Health Science Center at Houston. "Caregiving and Its Impact on the Workforce: Findings from the Bureau of National Affairs Survey." 1996.